Kundalini for Beginners

Meditations, Contexts, Methods and Effects

Contact: www.HarryEilenstein.de
Harry.Eilenstein@web.de
Harry Eilenstein at youtube

Production and publishing house: BoD – Books on Demand, Norderstedt

ISBN: 9783754312278

Table of Contents

I The History of Kundalini

Kundalini is not an Indian invention, but a universal phenomenon like telepathy, astrology or astral projection. Therefore, references to Kundalini can be found in many cultures – with the Indians (and later the Tibetans) having been the most thorough researchers, as with many magical-spiritual things.

This chapter, however, is not a detailed "History of Kundalini", but only a brief overview.

I 1. The Kundalini in the Palaeolithic Age

It can be assumed that the Kundalini was already well known in the Paleolithic Age, even though there is no direct evidence for it – there is, however, a very solid indirect evidence.

The oldest form of religion is shamanism – it goes back to at least the middle Paleolithic. A shaman is someone who has had a near-death and experienced during this leaving his body and floating above himself ("astral travel"). This experience has led to the realization that there is more than just the material body. This conscious leaving of one's own body is the origin of the conception of a soul, which received the form of a bird with all peoples due to the hovering with the astral body: the soul bird.

This soul bird may be a bird, a bird with a human head, a human with a birds head, a human with wings (angel), a human with a fether-garment, a human with fethers an his head etc.

Those who succeeded in recreating this experience at will were subsequently able to perceive other soul-birds (telepathically) and therefore became "soul-specialists".

When learning astral travel, one practices to become aware of one's own life force body and then to direct it purposefully – even outside of one's own physical body. However, becoming aware of one's own life force body is what one must first learn in awakening Kundalini as well.

The beginnings of the way of learning astral projection, the awakening of Kundalini and also hypnosis are identical: the awareness of one's own life force body.

Processes in the life force body				
		Goal		
		Astral journey	*Kundalini*	*Hypnosis*
aware-ness of the life force body	1st step	come to rest (sit or lie down)	come to rest (sit or lie down)	"Sit down."
	2nd step	relax	relax	"You are relaxed."
	3rd step	the experience of heaviness	the experience of heaviness	"You are heavy."
	4th step	the experience of warmth	the experience of warmth	"You are getting warm."
action with the life force body	5th step	the experience of vibrating with 6Hz	the experience of pulsa-tion, tingling, heat, etc.	"You are getting tired."
	6th step	movements of individual limbs (arm, leg, etc.) of the astral body and/or swaying of the astral body as in a high swell (one experiences this as supposed movements of the physical body)	turning and writhing in the root chakra (Kundalini snake)	"You fall asleep."
	7th step	conscious leaving of the physical body	the experience of the Kundalini rising from the root chakra to the crown chakra	the hypnotist takes over the function of the awake conscious-ness of the hypnotized

Because of this close connection between astral projection, which is the basis of the oldest and worldwide spread form of religion, i.e. shamanism, the shamans must have discovered the Kundalini fire early on while learning the astral journey – a good half of the way to both experiences consists in the awareness of one's own life force body.

The shamans therefore not only master the astral journey, but also know the Kundalini fire – and this knowledge goes back at least to the middle Old Stone Age to the origin of shamanism.

I 2.   The Kundalini in the Neolithic Age

At the beginning of the Neolithic Age, around 10,000 B.C., the temples of Göbekli Tepe, Nevali Cori, Jericho, etc. were built in northern Mesopotamia. In them there are some representations of the Kundalini – especially a head sculpture with ascending snake. There are also stone totem poles, reliefs on temple pillars, carvings on stone slabs, etc., on which snakes have been depicted, some of which are recognizable as Kundalini.

On these stone totem poles and temple columns also soul birds have been depicted. Among other things, the soul bird is found as a bird sitting on the neck of a person and looking forward over his head. Exactly the same representation can be found 7000 years later in a statue of the pharaoh Khafre, who built one of the pyramids of Giza.

These soul bird statues are found all over the world as totem poles: the pole itself is a human being and the bird on top of this pole is his soul bird. The oldest representation of such a soul bird originates from the cave paintings of Lascaux.

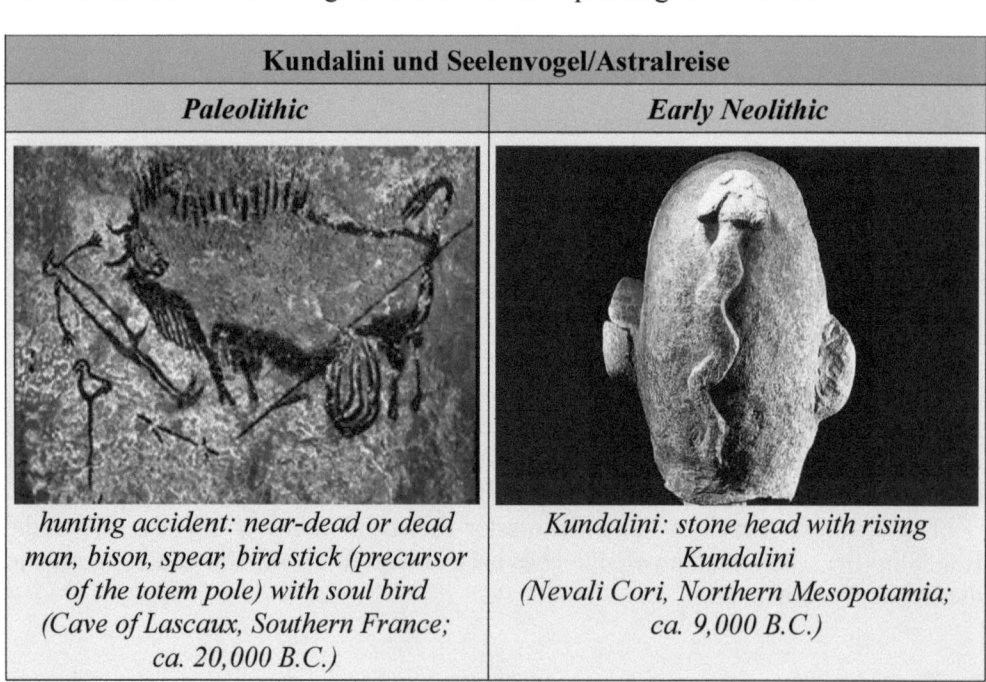

Kundalini und Seelenvogel/Astralreise	
Paleolithic	*Early Neolithic*
hunting accident: near-dead or dead man, bison, spear, bird stick (precursor of the totem pole) with soul bird (Cave of Lascaux, Southern France; ca. 20,000 B.C.)	*Kundalini: stone head with rising Kundalini (Nevali Cori, Northern Mesopotamia; ca. 9,000 B.C.)*

I 3.   The Kundalini among the Indo-Europeans

Around 7000 B.C. the ancestors of the Indo-Germans moved from northern Meso-potamia over the Caucasus to the southern Russian steppes, taking with them the world view of Göbekli Tepe, Nevali Cori, etc., thus also the knowledge of the Kundalini and astral travel.

From 2800 B.C. they have divided themselves into individual peoples. Of these Indo-Germanic individual peoples, the Indians have most systematically researched the experience of the rising Kundalini fire. Therefore, when we hear the word "kundalini" today, we think mainly of India – the word itself originates from India.

But also among the Celts the Kundalini was well known, as for example the report of the battle ecstasy of the hero Cú Chulain shows, who was the son of the sun god Lugh. In the relevant account in the Irish national epic "The Cattle Raid of Cuailgne", especially the rising and the heat are impressively described. The battle ecstasy was an application of the awakened Kundalini to battle magic.

The Celtic shaman god Cernunnos is also accompanied by a horned serpent ("dragon"). This motif is also found in Mesopotamia: The sun-god Marduk is accompanied by a horned serpent.

With the Teutons likewise the fight ecstasy is described, which was developed obviously by these two most western peoples of the Indo-Europeans. However, among the Teutons there are also representations of Kundalini outside of the martial ecstasy.

Several Kundalini Representations

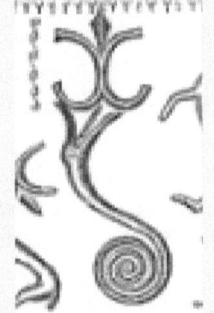

stylized man and Kundalini under root chakra (golden horn of Gallehus, Denmark; 400 A.D.)

man with Kundalini snake under root chakra (Isle of Man; Great Britain; ca. 950 A.D.)

Helmet with snake crawling over the head to the third eye (Sweden; ca. 700 A.D.)

Cernunnos (Gundestrup Cauldron, Denmark; 400 B.C.)

Marduk with horned dragon (Mesopotamia, ca. 2500 B.C.)

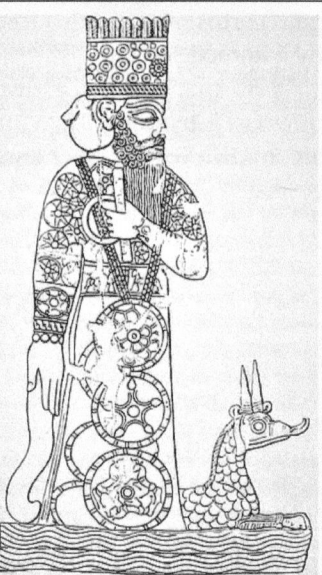

Marduk with horned dragon (Mesopotamia, ca. 2500 B.C.)

10

I 4.   The Kundalini in Central America

Among the Toltecs, Aztecs, Mayas and some other peoples in Central America, Quetzalcoatl is one of the most important deities. This god has the form of a snake covered with the blue feathers of the Quetzal bird. His name means "feathered snake."

Thus, he is a snake/bird hybrid, as also found among the Chinese as a flying dragon and in Europe as a winged dragon. This mythical creature originated from the connection of the ancestor snake or the Kundalini snake with the soul bird. In many cases this hybrid creature has been associated with fire and can, for example, breath fire.

Among the Aztecs he is depicted as a snake behind a man with a jaguar mask, i.e. behind a shaman. He was the protective deity of the Aztec priests and also the guardian of knowledge. He was considered by them as the "wisest man", i.e. he knows the afterlife and therefore also magic.

Quetzalcoatl was also the wind god. The wind was associated with the breath and with almost all peoples also with the life and therefore also with the soul – thus in the old testament the wind and the soul are called both "ruach" and with the Teutons Tyr was as beyond god also the "breath king", i.e. the soul king.

With the Toltecs "Quetzalcoatl" was also a military rank – were there also with the Toltecs ekstasy warriors?

Quetzalcoatl	

Kundalini behind shaman with jaguar mask (Aztecs, 900 BC)	*Vision serpent showing the underworld (Mayas, ca. 400 A.D.)*

11

15. The Kundalini with Other Peoples

Since both astral projection and Kundalini are among the basic magical-spiritual experiences, there are more or less clear references to them in many traditions.

Often, however, it is not possible to say exactly what the history of this tradition is, which is mainly due to the fact that these experiences can always be discovered anew independently of a tradition.

Astral projection will have been known early in the Paleolithic period due to the frequent near-death experiences at that time. Such faints, in which the soul (astral body) leaves the physical body, have also been observed in animals. However, the first concrete evidence of a soul bird is relatively recent: the bird on a staff in the Lascaux cave, painted about 22,000 years ago.

However, it is probable that already around 50,000 B.C. there will have been clear ideas not only about the astral body ("soul bird"), but also about the Kundalini. At this time lived in Eurasia the Homo erectus and the Neanderthal man, to which from Africa the Homo sapiens had migrated. From the cultural synthesis of these three types of people a new culture was born, which among other things brought forth goddess statuettes, musical instruments, cave paintings, soul bird representations, totem poles and probably also a more detailed study of Kundalini.

These elements are not to be found at all or only in very small traces in Africa, from where the Homo sapiens originates – if one disregards once the general Schamanism and the mother goddess, which presumably go back to the earliest Old Stone Age more than one million years ago. This speaks for the fact that the above-mentioned elements developed only by the culture synthesis 50,000 years ago.

Of course, it could be that some of these elements already existed before 50,000 B.C. in Homo erectus and Neanderthal man, but there are no concrete traces of this. However, altars, cult bull skulls, the storage of human skulls etc. are known from Homo erectus, which are 300,000 years old. Also the sweat lodges originate presumably at least from the middle Old Stone Age before approx. 600,000 years – they are likewise an "invention" of Homo erectus. The Neanderthals already created ritual stone circles in caves 180,000 years ago. Religion is thus already clearly older than the younger Old Stone Age, which began 50,000 years ago.

The Indians are also descended from this mixed culture which was mainly Homo erectus and Homo sapiens, which originated 50,000 years ago. The ancestors of the Indians migrated around 14,000 B.C. from northeast Asia over the Bering Strait land bridge, which was dry during the ice age, to northwest Alaska and then further down to Tierra del Fuego.

Of course, these considerations do not prove that Kundalini has been known for about 50,000 years (or more), but this date has at least some probability, since Kundalini has a close resemblance in Eurasia, America and Australia, but is largely absent in Africa. It could of course also go back to a tradition of Homo erectus, who lived in Eurasia, and then be clearly older than "only" 50,000 years.

I 6. Kundalini and Combat Ecstasy

The battle ecstasy is quite certainly a further development of the shamanic ecstasy, which served the afterlife journey. It is found among the Teutons and Celts and possibly also among the Toltecs (which, however, is quite uncertain). This application of Kundalini is at the most 2000 years old.

In principle, two elements of the free-flowing Kundalini are used in martial ecstasy: on the one hand, one-pointedness and, on the other, the power of Kundalini itself. The battle ecstatics, who were called "Berserker" ("bear-skin-men") or Ulfhedinn ("wolf-skin-men") by the Germanic tribes, used different methods of ecstasy like stomping, roaring or biting into the edge of the shield to put themselves into an "extraordinary state", by which they became insensitive to weapons and fire and received powers far beyond the normal measure.

- - -

The background of the history of religion and magic has only been briefly sketched here, as it is not the main concern of this small introduction to the phenomena and methods of Kundalini meditations.

I have presented some aspects in more detail in the following books:

Kundalini in general:
   "Kundalini I" and "Kundalini II"
general symbolism of Kundalini:
   "Drachenfeuer"
Kundalini in the early Neolithic Age:
   "Göbekli Tepe"
symbolism of Kundalini among the Germanic peoples:
   "Die Götter der Germanen, Band 64a: Magie und Ritual I"
   "Die Götter der Germanen, Band 42a: Die Symbolik der Schlangen und Drachen"
symbolism of Kundalini among the Celts:
   "Cernunnos"

II The Character of Kundalini

In order to assess the importance of Kundalini for one's own life, it is necessary to understand as accurately as possible what Kundalini actually is.

II 1. Life Force

Kundalini is not a physical organ or a physical process – it is a process in the realm of the life force.

So what is the life force? It is generally treated as a "non-physical substance" – although it is called a "force". Probably it is most precise to understand the life force as the phenomena at the border between consciousness and matter. One can use the life force to describe all processes in which consciousness acts directly on matter: telepathy, telekinesis, magic, meditation, ghosts, spirit healings, miracles, and so on. This fact alone suggests that the life force should be understood as an image that serves to describe the processes at the transition from consciousness to matter.

II 2. Chakras

The life force is not structureless, but forms certain structures which can be observed in consciousness as well as in nature – as one should expect from a "substance" which describes the transition between consciousness and matter. If the life force would not form structures and processes which can be found in consciousness as well as in matter, it could not describe the boundary and the connection between consciousness and matter.

The most important structure that the life force forms in the human body are the chakras. They are, so to speak, the life force organs in man. This is a complex system, but for the time being only the seven main chakras are important.

These seven chakras are part of one system in a simple way:

- At the center is the <u>heart chakra</u>, which contains a person's identity. This corresponds to the deep sleep consciousness that can be consciously reached in silent meditation. The heart chakra corresponds to the genital level with Sigmund Freud.

- Downward follow three chakras that relate to one's own body; upward follow three chakras that relate to the environment.

- Below the heart chakra is the <u>solar plexus</u> and above the heart chakra is the <u>throat chakra</u>. These two chakras are ideally the uninhibited physical self-expression (solar plexus) and the uninhibited social self-expression (throat chakra). It is in these two chakras, which correspond to the dream state and in which the emotions are found. They can be explored by dream journeys. This is the first concretization step of identity in the heart chakra: identity becomes impulses. With Freud, they correspond to the phallic level.

- Below and above these two chakras are the <u>hara</u> (below) and the <u>third eye</u> (above). The hara turns the physical impulses of the solar plexus into an inner support, a point of view, and a concrete desire; the third eye directs the social impulses toward concrete goals. These two chakras are the waking consciousness and the thinking. They correspond to the anal level with Freud.

- Finally, below the hara is the <u>root chakra</u>, which is responsible for physical contact, and above the third eye is the <u>crown chakra</u>, which is responsible for mental contact. This is where the concrete experience arises, which is why these two chakras are associated with the state of ecstasy – which is obvious with the lower chakra due to its proximity to sexuality. They correspond to the oral level with Freud.

Kundalini is a process within this life force anatomy in one's own body.

15

II 3.   Flow of Life Force

The seven major chakras and the various minor chakras are the organs of the life force body. In it, however, there are also processes which may be conceived, for the most part, as the flow of the life-force in this "anatomical system".

The "veins" in which this life force flows are an important part of yoga and many "life force healing" practices such as acupuncture.

The "main vein" runs from the root chakra straight up in the center of the body to the crown chakra – it is called the "sushumna" in yoga. To its left and right are the two main "secondary veins" – they are called "Ida" and Pingala". The Sushumna is connected to the image of one's soul; Ida and Pingala are connected to the image of one's inner whole man and inner whole woman.

Other "life force veins" are the nadis from yoga and the acupuncture meridians from traditional Chinese medicine.

One can compare the flow of life force in the life force body roughly to the circulation of blood in the physical body and also to the digestion system.

This life force flow is on the one hand a convection flow, that is, a circular flow – just as the blood circulation is such a convection flow. The life force rises in the center of the body like the jet of a fountain, unfolds above the crown chakra like the fountain of a waterspout fountain, and then flows outside the body like the drops of a fountain back down to the root chakra, from where the life force then rises again inside the body. This rising part of the life force flow is what is called "Kundalini" or "rising Kundalini fire".

This life force flow is on the other hand a straight flow, that is a flow that passes throught the life force body – like the food in the digestion system.

At the end of this book there will be some more details about this twofold system of life force currents in the body.

The system of chakras and "life force veins" is even more complex than it has been presented here, but this simple version is sufficient for now to be able to sketch the essence of Kundalini.

A detailed description may be found in my book "The Chakra System with the Minor Chakras".

II 4. The Functions of Kundalini

On its way from the root chakra to the crown chakra, the Kundalini flows through all seven main chakras. Obviously, one of the functions of Kundalini is to connect the seven chakras and also to carry the information in them to the outside when it flows back down outside the body at the outer edge of the life force body ("aura").

Some other functions of Kundalini will be discussed later when we look at the dynamics and action of the awakened Kundalini and the phenomena that occur when the flow of Kundalini is blocked.

II 5.   The Kundalini and the Heart Chakra

In the life force body there are at least two dynamics, which obviously have different tasks, otherwise they would not both exist:

- In the heart chakra lies the identity, which gradually becomes concrete experiences through the three pairs of chakras: Identity (heart chakra) first becomes feelings and impulses (solar plexus and throat chakra), then concrete intentions and ideas (hara and third eye), and finally concrete actions and experiences in the here and now (crown chakra and root chakra).

Thus, from the heart chakra emanates a radiance that carries identity out into the world. Ideally, you express exactly who you really are by every action and every attitude.

This works also in the other direction: From the contact in the two outer chakras (crown chakra and root chakra) arise insights in the two middle chakras (hara and third eye) and then feelings in the two inner chakras (solar plexus and throat chakra), that become consious in the centre (heart chakra).

The heart chakra leads to the urge to express and experience one's innermost being on the outside.

- The flow of life force, of which Kundalini is the ascending part, connects all chakras and ensures a constant exchange between them. It also ensures that all the contents of the chakras, i.e. all the images in the psyche also reach the outer surface of the life force body ("aura"), where they attract the appropriate experiences. This is, among other things, the basis for magic, in which events are summoned by the imagination of images. In the same way, however, the fears, addictions and self-doubts in one's own psyche also summon the events in the outside world that match them.

The flowing of the Kundalini thus ensures that all contents of the chakras and thus of the psyche are integrated into an overall attitude and that these contents are also carried outward to the "skin" of the life force body, where they summon like "sockets" the "plugs" that fit them. This has the effect that one experiences one's own inner state on the outside.

The flow of the Kundalini thus leads to a reflection of the inner in the outer.

The heart chakra and the Kundalini respectively the entire life force circuit work together and lead to the fact that one finds oneself mirrored in one's experiences and realizes one's own nature by this. These processes make it also possible to express one's own essence (soul in the heart chakra) more and more clearly and purely and intensely.

18

III   The Kundalini and the Physical Body

The chakras are often considered the "inside" or the "life force aspect" of certain organs. Accordingly, Kundalini would then also have to be the life force equivalent of, for example, the digestive system.

III 1.   Kundalini, Chakras and Organs

If we look at the connection between the chakras and the organs, and also if we look more closely at the connection between the Kundalini and the digestive system, we notice that much, but by no means everything, corresponds. So there seems to be a connection, but it cannot be a simple equation of the chakras with the organs.

If we trace the anatomy of man back through the apes, the early mammals, the reptiles, the amphibians and the fishes to the unicellular organisms, we can see that some organs have acquired new functions in the course of evolution, that other organs have migrated to another place in the body and that there have been some other forms of organ change.

The further one goes back in the history of the anatomy of living beings into the past, the better the functions of the organs correspond to the character of the chakras located at the respective place in the body. In the first, simple living beings, a complete correspondence can be found between the character of the chakras and the function of the organs.

Since the chakras are the "organs" of the life force and the life force is the transition from consciousness to matter, one should expect that the first living beings still corresponded in their structure to the structure of the chakras – which is indeed the case.

The same applies to the Kundalini, i.e. to the entire life force flow in the body, which corresponds to the digestive system.

The more exact details are not important for the understanding of Kundalini. The findings show above all that the conception of the life force as the boundary area between consciousness and matter (body) is correct.

If necessary, the details may be found in my book "Chakras und Organe".

III 2. Brain Structure and Meditation Posture

The brain is very complex, but by no means chaotically structured. On the surface of the cerebrum ("cortex") there are areas corresponding to the individual body parts, which process the perceptions of these organs and send movement impulses to them.

These body areas are arranged on the cortex in a specific order consisting of four areas that follow one another. This arrangement is as follows:

> 1. genitals
> 2. toes – feet – legs – body (outside) – neck – head
> 3. shoulders – arms – hands – fingers
> 4. eyes – nose – lips – teeth – tongue – throat – intestines

The life force flow, of which Kundalini is the ascending part, corresponds largely to this sequence:

> 1. ascending (Kundalini): body to head
> 2. descending: eyes to intestines / shoulders to fingers

This correspondence is not perfect, but at least fitting ro an extent that cannot be a pure coincidence.

So this finding corresponds to the previous consideration about the correspondence between the chakras and the organs or the correspondence between the life force circulation and the blood circulation respectively the life force rising and the digestive system.

From the discrepancies between the arrangement of the body parts on the cerebrum cortex and the flow of the life force in the body, a posture can be derived, which is also the basic posture in Kundalini Yoga. It will be described later in this book.

IV   The Dynamics of Kundalini

Kundalini has a distinct dynamic, the knowledge of which can facilitate the awakening of Kundalini – and above all give a little orientation. This dynamic is, of course, closely related to the momentum of the life force and also to the structures that it forms on its own.

IV 1.   Chakras

The easiest way to see the basic structure of the life force body is through the system of chakras, which is completely symmetrical:

The Symmetry of the Chakras I							
Area	**Chakra**	**Quality**	**Sigmund Freud**	**Symmetry**			
outside	crown chakra	spiritual contact	oral phase				
	third eye	mental form = orientation	anal phase				
	throat chakra	social self-expression	phallic phase				
center	heart chakra	identity	genital phase				
inside	solar plexus	physical self-expression	phallic phase				
	hara	physical form = inner support	anal phase				
	root chakra	physical contact	oral phase				

The six intermediate chakras, which lie between the seven main chakras, are also important for the consideration of Kundalini. The seven main chakras can be thought of as the capitals of seven kingdoms. Between each of these seven kingdoms there is a boundary wall, but it has a gate: the six intermediate chakras. When there is a blockage in the life force, the blockage is in these six intermediate chakras: then at least one of the six gates is closed.

With the six intermediate chakras, the symmetry of the chakra system is very clear:

- The central kingdom is the chest, that is, the area of the body enclosed by the ribs. In its center lies the <u>heart chakra</u> as the "capital".

At the lower end of the sternum lies the <u>wish tree intermediate chakra</u>, where identity is transformed into general, physical desires.

At the upper end of the sternum lies the <u>thymus intermediate chakra</u> that transforms identity into general, social desires.

The ribs are the innermost area of protection.

- The two kingdoms below and above the chest are the kingdom of the <u>solar plexus</u> and the kingdom of the <u>throat chakra</u>.

The solar plexus kingdom is bounded above by the wish tree intermediate chakra. Downward, it is bounded by the intermediate chakra of internal nourishment (before birth): the <u>umbilical intermediate chakra</u> (nourishment through the umbilical cord before birth).

The kingdom of the throat chakra is bounded below by the thymus intermediate chakra. Upwards it is limited by the intermediate chakra of external nourishment (after birth): the <u>palatal intermediate chakra</u>.

Nourishment is an exchange with the environment.

- The two kingdoms below and above these three middle kingdoms are the kingdom of the <u>hara</u> and the kingdom of the <u>third eye</u>.

The hara kingdom is bounded above by the umbilical intermediate chakra. Downward, it is bounded by the <u>pubic hair intermediate chakra</u>.

The third eye kingdom is bounded below by the palatal intermediate chakra. Upward, it is bounded by the <u>main hair intermediate chakra</u>.

The hair is an outer protection.

This symmetry becomes clearer when it is represented graphically:

Area	Chakra	Quality	Sigmund Freud	Symmetry		
outside	crown chakra	spiritual contact	oral phase			
	main hair intermediate chakra (hair)					
	third eye	mental form = orientation	anal phase			
	palatal intermediate chakra (food)					
	throat chakra	social self-expression	phallic phase			
	thymus intermediate chakra (ribs)					
centre	heart chakra	identity	genital phase			
onside	*wish tree intermediate chakra (ribs)*					
	solar plexus	physical self-expression	phallic phase			
	umbilical intermediary chakra (food)					
	hara	physical form = inner support	anal phase			
	pubic hair intermediary chakra (hair)					
	root chakra	physical contact	oral phase			

The Symmetry of the Chakras II

IV 2. Solar System

If the life force should have a general dynamic and a structure resulting from this dynamic, then this structure should also be found in matter – especially in the very simplest forms, since this presumed life force structure cannot yet have been super-imposed there by later developments.

The most impressive example is our sun or more generally a star (a sun in another planetary system) as well as the surrounding space formed by it. There you can find exactly the same dynamics and structure as in the chakra system.

- The center is the sun – in it the heat and the light originate and it contains by far the largest part of the mass of the entire solar system.
It corresponds to the heart chakra.

- The sun radiates not only light and heat, but also ions into its surrounding space. These ions collide with the stardust, which is made up of single atoms and fine dust, and is distributed throughout the galaxy to which our sun belongs. The ions coming from the sun push this stardust away from the sun, forming a region all around the sun that is completely dominated by the solar ions, which are somewhat poetically called "solar wind".
This area corresponds to the uninhibited self-expression of the solar plexus and the throat chakra.

- The solar wind pushes the stardust further and further outward – just as a snow pusher pushes the snow in front of it. This creates a spherical "wall" around the sun, which is now well outside the orbit of Pluto. This "wall" consists of the stardust and the solar ions which have been pushed away from the solar orbit. But although this hollow sphere-shaped "wall" is only a dense dust cloud, it has altogether about the same mass as the earth. This "wall" is mostly called "shock front".
This area corresponds to the structure and boundary of the hara and the third eye.

- The shock front expands and the sun moves through the galaxy. This means that the spherical shock front around the sun moves like a ship through the sea of stardust. In front of every ship there is a bow wave – it is the place where ship and water meet. Such a bow wave also exists in front of the shock front.
This area corresponds to the contact with the environment through the root

chakra and the crown chakra.

- The sun contains ions (electrically charged particles) and moves. A moving electrical charge causes a magnetic field to be created. In addition to its movement through the galaxy, the sun also rotates on its axis. A rotation compresses the magnetic field into two beams that emerge through the two poles of the rotation axis rotation – these are the north pole and the south pole in the case of the Earth. These two rays are called "jets" – they extend far beyond the solar system itself into space.

In the chakra system, these two jets correspond to the sushumna, which projects upward and downward from the heart chakra. The sushumna is the central life force channel along which the seven main chakras are lined up – the sushumna also passes through the gates of the six intermediate chakras.

- At these two jets, ions fly outward, accelerated by the magnetic field. Since there are two different electrical charges, these ions are also accelerated in two different ways: a clockwise spiral and a counterclockwise spiral out into space.

In the chakra system, these two spirals correspond to Ida and Pingala, which are the two life force channels located next to the sushumna that cross at each chakra – they look like two counter-rotating spirals (3D representation); if they are viewed from the side: two serpentine lines that regularly cross at the chakras (2D representation).

- In the sun, nuclear fusion takes place in the center, generating great heat. The matter heated in the core of the sun rises to the surface of the sun, because hot matter is lighter than cooler matter. At the surface of the sun, this matter then cools down again and sinks back into the center of the sun.

This convection current ("circular current") corresponds to the convection current of the life force in the human bod: it flows outward from the heart chakra as impulses to the three pairs of the six outer chakras, and a second flow returns back from the six outer chakras to the heart chakra as perceptions of the world.

Kundalini is an aspect of these dynamics of the life force. Both this dynamic and this basic structure characterize not only the life force (and therefore consciousness), but also the simple forms of matter.

IV 3. Vajra

Vajra

This basic structure is also found in religion as a symbol; the Vajra, i.e. the "thunderbolt" from the Indo-Tibetan symbolism.

This symbol has been originally a symbol of the lightning of the sky god in Neolithic Mesopotamia. It gradually evolved and finally became the complex Indo-Tibetan symbol of the innermost being of the world.

The vajra is structured like the chakra system and the solar system:

In the center is a sphere – the center: the heart chakra and the sun, respectively.

The sphere is followed by two lotus flowers – the first stage of unfoldment: the solar plexus and the throat chakra or the area of the solar wind.

The lotus blossoms are followed by the heads of the four elephants representing the four elements – the second stage of unfoldment: the hara and the third eye or the shock front.

The elephant heads are followed by the elephant trunks – the third unfoldment stage: the root chakra and the crown chakra or the bow wave.

IV 4.   Crop Circles

In the crop circles, the "polar unfolding out of a center" is the most important basic structure that can be found in many crop circles.

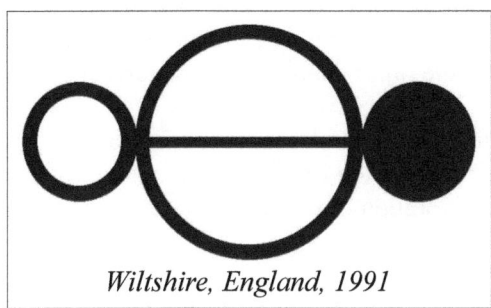
Wiltshire, England, 1991

This crop circle from Wiltshire in South England, has a clearly polar structure: an open circle, a closed circle as well as a connecting line and a central circle.

This corresponds to the astrological sign for the opposition aspect, i.e. for the complementary opposition: ☍

In this crop circle, the ring on the left side, when you enter it, feels like a mountain top – the circle area on the right side, however, feels like a cave. This contrast could also be described as radiating and sucking, outside and inside, light and dark etc.. This confirms the interpretation of this structure as a complementary opposition.

On the line between these two poles a great, constant tension could be felt – just what one would expect between two poles.

However, the large ring in the middle felt different at each point and the same point was not the same even after three minutes. This is because something is flowing, circling, pulsating, rotating in this ring – presumably the life force.

This three-part, polar structure reminds, among other things, of Rudolf Steiner's threefold structure: a pole that solidifies ("Ahriman"), a pole that dissolves ("Lucifer"), and in between a pulsating system ("Christ").

The ring in the center is also the zodiac along which the planets move, with two signs opposite each other on the zodiac (astrological opposition) also having opposite but complementary qualities.

This structure is thus also a variant of the yin/yang sign: ☯ The two poles represent the primordial opposition of yin and yang, as well as the eternal change that arises by them and that is described in the I Ching ("Book of Changes").

27

IV 5. The Whole State

These considerations show that the life force, when it can unfold unhindered, assumes a certain structure in which there is an inner dynamic – the convection current.

This structure in man is the seven main chakras plus the six intermediate chakras. The dynamics in this structure is, on the one hand, the radiance of the center (heart chakra → root chakra /crown chakra) and, on the other hand, the rising current of the life force (Kundalini).

Therefore, the most wholesome and therefore the most pleasant state is the unimpeded radiance of the center and the unimpeded flow of the life force. The pursuit of the awakening of Kundalini is consequently the restoration of the whole state and thus the most comprehensive self-healing conceivable.

One can also strive for a Kundalini experience simply out of curiosity, but with that one would not have exhausted the potential of Kundalini by far …

V The Variety of Kundalini Experiences

There are various experiences associated with Kundalini, of which the "inner fire" is the most characteristic experience. As with just about everything in the lives of people, there are various influences that help shape these experiences and give them an individual coloring, so to speak.

V 1. Culture and Tradition

In countries like India or Tibet, in whose religion Kundalini is an integral part, it is naturally easy to classify Kundalini phenomena and also to receive knowledgeable comments about them. Of course, these comments are usually colored by the religious evaluation of these phenomena.

In the field of Christian religion, on the other hand, a Kundalini tradition is almost completely absent. Therefore, Kundalini phenomena have been viewed there with skepticism at best.

In Central America, Kundalini was associated primarily with the shamans and with the snake god Quetzalcoatl.

Thus, in every culture there is a certain classification and evaluation of Kundalini, ranging from "desirable" to "better avoid" and "highly dangerous" to "devil's work". These cultural and therefore collective evaluations are often internalized and unconscious, but one will have to deal with them when one starts to deal with Kundalini.

For example, it will not be easy for a Christian, for whom the snake is the symbol of the devil par excellence, to imagine or experience the Kundalini snake in himself and to understand it as a symbol of the life force, that is, to equate it with the Holy Spirit and thus as a part of God …

V 2. Horoscope

"Every Jeck is different ..." as they say so wisely in the Rhineland. ("Jeck" = carnival participant).

This is impressively confirmed by astrology. Unless you meet someone who was born at the same moment in approximately the same place, you will not find anyone who works exactly like you. Everyone has a different horoscope and therefore a different character, a different psyche – and also a different experience of Kundalini.

This experience is to a large extent influenced by the position of the moon in the horoscope, since this symbolizes the life force. However, Kundalini also has connections with all the other planets, as Mars is a force, as the Sun leads to radiance, as Pluto is the existential, and so on.

Therefore, it is necessary to find out the method that is suitable for oneself. Of course, there are generalities – for example, everyone has seven main chakras – but one should not underestimate the individual differences and always take it into account in all Kundalini meditations.

Thus in this book I can only present my view of the Kundalini, which will probably not completely coincide with the view of anyone else – but in spite of all differences we can also give each other suggestions, because we all live in the same world and the whole diversity is based on the same basic principles ... everyone has a Kundalini, because otherwise he would not live ...

V 3. Blockages

The differences in the experience of Kundalini are to a very large extent also due to the state of one's own psyche. If everything is in balance, it is quite easy to awaken the Kundalini; if there are blockages in the psyche, it is already more difficult; and if there should be one or more traumas, the awakening of the Kundalini will probably either not be easy or a little unpleasant.

However, awakening the Kundalini is a very good way to raise awareness and heal such blockages and traumas – and self-healing is ultimately the only real reason why it might be worthwhile to awaken one's own Kundalini. Of course, pure curiosity and thirst for knowledge is also a good motivation, but this does not exhaust the full potential of Kundalini awakening.

The blockages are located at the six intermediate chakras – sometimes one of these six gates is partially or completely blocked. In this case, there is a lack of life force in the main chakra, which is located behind this intermediate chakra gate, as seen from the heart chakra. In the opposite pole to this "deficiency chakra" there is then a life force congestion – the intermediate chakra in front of this main chakra is also partially or completely blocked.

However, the attitude in the two intermediate chakras is different: One intermediate chakra is kept closed out of fear of allowing life force to flow into the chakra behind it (life force deficiency), while the other intermediate chakra is closed out of an effort to keep all life force in the chakra behind it (life force congestion).

This leads to the fact that in the case of a blockage always two chakras are affected:

    1. oral level: root chakra and crown chakra
       healed state: security
       sick state: lack

        the sick polarity is:

        (a) life force congestion in the root chakra
           life force deficiency in the crown chakra
             => **addict**

        or the polarity is the other way around:

        b) life force congestion in the crown chakra
           life force deficiency in the root chakra
             => **ascetic**

2. <u>anal level</u>: hara and third eye
   healed state: strength
   sick state: fear

      the sick polarity is:

      a) life force congestion in the hara
         life force deficiency in the third eye
            => **perpetrator**

      or the polarity is the other way around:

      b) life force congestion in the third eye.
         life force deficiency in the hara
            => **victim**

3. <u>phallic level</u>: solar plexus and throat chakra
   healed state: self-love
   sick state: self-doubt

      the sick polarity is:

      (a) life force congestion in the solar plexus.
         life force deficiency in the throat chakra
            => **star** (megalomania)

      or the polarity is exactly the other way around:

      b) life force congestion in the throat chakra.
         life force deficiency in the solar plexus
            => **fan** (inferiority complex)

These are the three levels on which a blockage may be found – each time occurring in two opposite orientations.

(A detailed description may be found in my book "The Chakra System with the Minor Chakras").

V 4. Method

The experience of Kundalini also depends on the method of its awakening. For example, its spontaneous awakening without one's own doing is something that can be quite disturbing – one probably no longer has the feeling of having everything under control and being able to direct everything.

Similarly, if the Kundalini is unintentionally awakened by drugs or by certain meditation techniques, one knows what the trigger has been, but may still be a little helpless in the face of the phenomena.

Finally, there are also different methods of intentional awakening of the Kundalini – this intention also has a great influence on the experience.

The "Indian style" is to "light a fire under your butt" by breathing exercises and the like, whereby the Kundalini awakens and begins to rise, causing you to gradually to become aware of all your repressed fears, addictions, angers, pains, etc. in your own psyche and body. With this method, one simply endures these feelings and continues to meditate until these feelings eventually fade away.

The "tantric style" also creates "fire under the butt" by using sexuality to stimulate the root chakra. However, this sexual tension is not discharged by orgasm, but held until the life force finds another path to move along, and then rises up through the sushumna.

The "moral style" consists of behaving in an exemplary way oneself, by which the chakras then develop and eventually the blockages dissolve. Whether this style, which is represented today above all by anthroposophists, actually works, is not quite certain, since it presupposes that one has actually recognized precisely what is salutary, right, moral, ethical, etc. – and with these subjects there is certainly more than one opinion about what is right.

The "psychological style" is based on healing the psyche: the more blockages are dissolved, the freer the Kundalini may flow.

Besides these approaches, there are many other methods and also many mixed forms such as "drugs and teachers", "meditation and tantra" or "psychotherapy and meditation".

V 5. Beyond Healing

First of all, there are the phenomena that occur in the awakening of Kundalini and in the healing of the life force body, that is, in the healing of the chakras and the psyche. However, this does not exhaust the possibilities of Kundalini experiences – basically, these possibilities really unfold after the awakening of Kundalini. Kundalini awakening is not only about the healing itself, but above all about the subsequent life in the healed state.

By the healing of the life force body, one achieves the possibility of using the life force to a far greater extent than before. These possibilities are known in India as "siddhis"; in Christian culture they are usually called "miracles". The awakened Kundalini enables more extensive and profound forms of magic.

Three phenomena often occur spontaneously when Kundalini awakens – they relate to breathing, sleeping, and eating, three basic functions or necessities of the body. When the Kundalini awakens, it happens that these three vital activities are suddenly no longer necessary.

The awakened Kundalini apparently directs the life force and keeps the body alive independently of breathing, sleeping and eating.

> The "no longer needing to sleep" is known especially from Tibet. It sometimes occurs initially as a change in sleep – there are longer periods during the night when one is "dreaming awake" or "sleeping awake", so to speak, i.e. when one is conscious while sleeping or dreaming. This is obviously a coordination of waking consciousness or subconsciousness (dream) with deep sleep consciousness.
>
> The same happens also with the dream journey (waking + dream), that is "conscious dreaming". This state of consciousness happens also with the silence meditation, with which the consciousness is without contents – one is just conscious of being conscious (waking + deep sleep), that is "conscious silence".
>
> The Kundalini thus seems to promote the integration of the different modes of consciousness – which is very plausible, since it rises through the seven chakras, which are connected with the four modes of consciousness (deep sleep: heart chakra; dream state/subconsciousness: solar plexus and throat chakra; waking consciousness: hara and third eye; ecstasy: root chakra and crown chakra).
>
> The intense happiness/love (Ananda) that sometimes occurs is probably the integration of the waking consciousness and the ecstatic state.

The occurrence of these three coordination effects is plausible, because when the Kundalini flows freely, the blockages must be dissolved, which in turn causes the individual parts of the psyche and thus the chakras to begin to cooperate with each other. Since the forms of consciousness are linked to the chakras and the Kundalini flows through the chakras, the integration of several forms of consciousness is almost inevitable.

The integration of the waking consciousness into the dreaming and into the deep sleep therefore leads to a "waking dreaming" and a "waking deep sleep" and finally probably to the fact that one no longer has a separate sleep state at all.

The "no longer needing to breathe" is known from some Indian yogis and Tibetan lamas – there are cases where yogis have allowed themselves to be buried for a month and then still lived afterwards. I also know a woman very well to whom I once showed a simple Kundalini meditation and who stopped breathing for 20 minutes right at the first attempt.

What happens at this is quite unclear from a physiological point of view, since these possibilities obviously override the usual laws of nature. However, the phenomenon seems to be quite similar to "not needing to sleep anymore".

The same is true for "no longer needing to eat", which for some years has been quite well known as "breatharianism".

Kundalini flows freely and unhindered when the chakras and thus the states of consciousness have been integrated – which also means that the psyche has been healed. Apparently, a healed psyche has abilities that go far beyond the "absence of disease".

It also fits well that shamans, magicians and miracle healers often have an awakened Kundalini. However, this fact can only be determined with certainty in India and Tibet – in other parts of the world one is mostly dependent on assumptions, because there the concept of Kundalini has often been formulated only very vaguely. Also the battle ecstasy belongs to this context – it is an external, battle-magical application of the rising Kundalini.

The connection between awakened Kundalini and genius, which has been observed many times, also belongs to the consequences of healed chakras and free flowing Kundalini.

Another phenomenon of the awakened Kundalini is the possibility of heating the body at will in such a way that one becomes insensitive to cold. For the Tibetan monks, who wear only a thin cotton robe in the icy cold of Tibet, this possibility of using awakened Kundalini has a distinct practical benefit.

VI Ways to Awaken Kundalini

In some people the Kundalini awakens spontaneously, which usually brings some confusion and a major crisis. However, there are ways to awaken the Kundalini consciously and intentionally. The list of these methods in this chapter is certainly not complete, but it will at least give a good overview of the different possible approaches.

As with just about everything, in awakening Kundalini one must see which mixture of approaches leads to a method that "tastes" good and is most effective for oneself.

VI 1. Life Force Pressure

Probably the most important and oldest approach is to gather life force in the root chakra from which the Kundalini rises in the center of the body. Since the life force is the perception of the boundary and transition between consciousness and matter, this accumulation of life force in the root chakra can be achieved simply by concentrating one's consciousness on the root chakra. When one's attention is focused on the root chakra, the consciousness concentrates on this "place," which in turn means that this part of the life force body comes into focus and is emphasized.

While this concentration can be completely formless, simply looking inwardly at one's own root chakra all the time and noticing it, usually this concentration is aided by external and internal aids. These aids are the mantra, breath control, imagination and body posture.

VI 1. a) Mantra

A mantra is a word or a short phrase that describes the goal to be achieved by this mantra. This mantra is spoken or chanted inwardly or outwardly by oneself. This can be done in the context of meditation but it can also be an accompaniment to everyday activities.

Chanting a mantra or a short song together, which is repeated constantly, can be extremely powerful, because the concentration of the participants, if it is high enough, supports each other.

The mantra is, so to speak, an "acoustic aid to concentration." The endless repetition of the mantra also creates an inner rhythm, a momentum, which has a coordinating effect on the psyche and thus increases concentration.

Concentration also has another effect: although one begins in the waking state, by concentration and vibration the contents of the psyche and the processes within it become organized, so that waking consciousness can expand to the dream state, deep sleep or the ecstatic state:

- The expansion to the dream state seems to occur especially when one chants a mantra alone and is completely focused on the subject in question, e.g., a deity. Then a dream journey arises out of the mantra chanting, in which one perceives inner images e.g. of a deity.

- The expansion to deep sleep state seems to be triggered by devotion to the subject, e.g. Shiva. Thereby an inner stillness, a being filled, a smile and radiance arises – and most of the time the mantra fades away quite unnoticed and one is simply present.

This state can become stable and self-sustaining, so that one needs a decision to leave it again (which, however, is not difficult).

- The extension to the ecstasy state seems to have a very high concentration and an inner longing, i.e. strong feelings, as its basis. In this state, one is completely focused, for example, on the deity – fixated on it, so to speak, out of free will. Thereby one reaches a higher and higher inner intensity and experiences e.g. the deity more and more intensely. The ecstatic state seems to be more easily attainable in groups than alone.

This, too, can eventually become a stable state by which one is carried and in which one can rest. Again, one needs a resolution to leave this state.

So the mantra is a general aid to concentration. When you focus concentration on the root chakra with the help of a mantra, you gather awareness there, you put the root chakra in the focus of awareness, making it emphasized and more active. This can eventually stimulate the root chakra to the point where the Kundalini begins to stir and rise.

One of the advantages of a mantra is that it can occupy the mind and significantly reduce its "inner self-talk" – which in turn increases concentration considerably.

Mantras that refer to the Kundalini such as "fire", "teja" (Sanskrit for "fire"), "Agni" (Indian god of fire), "Shiva" (Indian god of Kundalini), "Kundalini" etc. are suitable for a Kundalini mantra meditation. Probably it makes most sense to use the simplest word, i.e. the word for "fire" in one's native language.

VI 1. b) Breath Control

Breath control as a meditation aid is known mainly from India under the name "Pranayama". This technique has many aspects: The duration of breaths, the different durations of inhalation and exhalation, the manner of inhalation and exhalation (gentle, thrusting, sucking, etc.), breathing through the nose or mouth, closing one of the two nostrils while breathing, etc.

In addition, there are ideas about how to direct the breath through the body - imaginatively, for example, it can be directed to the abdomen or to the hand. Of course, it is only the life force and not the concrete air that one directs.

Furthermore, there is the long breath-holding and also hyperventilation ("rebirthing breath"), in which one breathes very quickly and deeply.

However, there are also simple forms of breath directing that are also very effective. If you use a mantra, you can do a simple breath/mantra meditation:

> - Inhale and imagine taking in life force while inhaling and directing it to the root chakra.

> - Exhaling and imagining the life force gathering and condensing in the root chakra and thus beginning to glow and radiate.

There are many more specific breath directing methods, but this is the basic and simplest method for awakening the Kundalini.

In all methods used to increase concentration on the root chakra, it is important not to focus so much on the method, such as the breath and the mantra, but to focus primarily on the root chakra. Sitting in silence with your consciousness firmly focused on your root chakra is quite sufficient – everything else is an aid to facilitate this concentration on the root chakra.

VI 1. c) Imagination

In the previous section, the imagination of directing the breath in the body has already been described. Such imaginations, that is, self-created inner images, are very often used in meditation. They range from the imagination of a point of light in the center of a chakra, to the imagination of taking the form of a deity ("invocation"), to walking in a large, complete mandala built like a city with a temple in its center.

The most important imagination related to the awakening of Kundalini is the idea that there is a fire burning in the root chakra. Since the life force is usually perceived as heat and sometimes as a glow, fire is a fitting image for this meditation. Therefore, one also speaks of "Kundalini fire", of the "rising heat" – and in some areas in West Africa, the life force is called "Kalifi", i.e. "fire of life".

In Kundalini meditation different symbols are used to concentrate on the root chakra, but they are all very similar:

- Very often the Tibetan symbol for the fire is used: a narrow, red triangle with its tip pointing upwards.

- There is also the possibility of using the Indian symbol for fire ("Teja-Tattwa"), which is an equilateral red triangle with its apex pointing upwards.

- The alchemical symbol for fire is also an equilateral triangle pointing upwards, but it has no color.

- One can also use a red tetrahedron as a fire symbol, that is, the Platonic solid whose surface consists of four equilateral triangles.

- Finally, one can also quite naturalistically imagine a flame in the root chakra.

As is generally sensible, one should see which symbol appeals to one the most, and then use this symbol.

Now, in meditation, three elements are already linked: mantra, breath control and imagination.

VI 1. d) Asana

One of the best known elements of meditation is the posture – the "asanas" of Hatha Yoga.

The oldest known posture in Kundalini Yoga is the "Dragon" – this name probably refers to the Kundalini, which is often represented as a snake (a dragon is a large snake). This posture is also called "Vir-Asana", which can be translated as "hero posture" or quite literally and somewhat less pathetically as "man posture".

This posture is quite simple: you sit on the ground with your legs folded underneath you, your buttocks on your heels, your legs in front of you, your knees all the way forward; you sit upright and either place your hands in your lap or raise them up next to your head in the classical way (upper arms to the side and slightly downward, lower arms vertically upward, hands upright, palms facing your head).

In this posture, the root chakra is emphasized by having the soles of the feet near the root chakra – in the simple version of this posture, the hands in the lap are also near the root chakra.

VI 1. e) Movement

There are also some meditations that involve movement. This may be a simple contemplative walking, or the asana of the "blossoming lotus," in which one uses arms and hands to represent the opening of a flower while seated, or the "sun salutation," which consists of a sequence of several yoga postures, etc.

However, there does not seem to be a specific sequence of movements for awakening the Kundalini. While performing the "blossoming lotus" asana, one can also imagine the Kundalini rising, but I am not aware that this would have a particularly beneficial effect.

VI 1. f) Motivation

One of the most important meditation fundamentals is one's own motivation for this meditation, i.e. for the goal to be achieved by this meditation. A single-minded motivation produces perfect concentration, and such concentration is perfectly sufficient for awakening the Kundalini in the root chakra. Unfortunately, one is rarely in such a one-pointed motivation, so that one needs all kinds of tools …

So it is useful to make clear why you actually want to do the Kundalini meditation. One has a high motivation e.g. if one is very ill and wants to heal oneself by awakening the Kundalini. Also the striving for power by the awakened Kundalini can be such a motivation – whereby the awakened Kundalini will usually have dissolved the original need for power by its rising. One can also simply be a very curious person who wants to experience something new. There are many possibilities here.

> Sometimes one also meets a suitable meditation form by chance, without even noticing that one is actually meditating. For example, during my community service, to which I rode by bicycle for a good hour, I got quite cold during this ride in winter – especially on my hands. Since I was learning magic at the time, I thought that I could just channel the fire element into my hands.
> For this I imagined drawing the fire element from the earth's core or from the engines of passing cars and directing it with my breath into my hands and letting it glow there. In doing so, I spoke "fire" inwardly as I breathed in and out. In addition, I brought the rhythm of my leg movements on the bicycle into harmony with my breath. Since I was able to keep my hands warm with this "bicycle meditation," I continued to perform this meditation with great concentration (and with great joy at its effectiveness).

40

Thus, I had a mantra, a breath guidance, an imagination, a movement and a very high and constant motivation, since it has been very cold this winter. Therefore, by this meditation, I very soon entered the ecstasy state, which feels like waking up from the normal waking state – it is warmth and smiles and happiness and love and being fulfilled …

The importance of one-pointed motivation and also the problems with this form of motivation has been well known to yogis, lamas and shamans. Therefore, for example, the Tibetan monks have thought of a little trick. If a Tibetan wants to become a lama (monk), he has to practice the Kundalini meditation, which is called "Tummo" in Tibet.

When he has prepared himself sufficiently, he must pass a test which consists of dipping his monk's robe in water five times during one night in the freezing cold in Tibet, putting it on and drying it by the heat of his Kundalini meditation. Due to the great cold, the one-directed motivation is no longer a problem in this meditation.

By this the monk also enters the state of ecstasy … which is ultimately the goal of this meditation …

These two examples show an essential quality of one-directed motivation: the knowledge of its effectiveness. When one has experienced that a method works, one applies it when necessary to achieve its effect. One-directed motivation, and therefore one-directed concentration, arises naturally when the person knows that his actions will be successful.

In general, one does not have to concentrate hard when, for example, one is hungry and wants to eat – one knows, when one is hungry, eating helps. The same is true for thirst and drinking, tiredness and sleeping, desire and sex, and many other things.

This natural motivation and concentration is also needed in meditation. Of course, this basis can only develop after one has had the experience that meditation has an effect.

VI 2.   Development of the Psyche

Kundalini is a part of the life force circuit in the life force body of man. The life force is the boundary and the transition between consciousness and matter – consequently, the Kundalini is a movement both in the consciousness and in the body. Since fears, addictions, repressed pains, depressions, traumas and the like are contents of the consciousness and also of the body, the Kundalini is closely connected with these structures in the consciousness and in the body of the human being.

Such rigid structures as fears, addictions, repressed pains, depressions, traumas and the like obviously stand in the way of the flow of Kundalini. The dissolving of such blockages therefore enables a freer flow of the life force and consequently the awakening of the Kundalini.

For this reason, healing the psyche and the body is also a way to bring Kundalini into flow. However, this does not necessarily mean that such healing must also lead to a conscious awareness of Kundalini. It does mean, however, that the awakening of the Kundalini necessarily leads to a perception of one's own blockages – no matter whether one begins with the awakening of the Kundalini and is thereby confronted with one's own blockages, or whether one begins e.g. a psychotherapy and thereby finds and experiences these blockages.

One can therefore assume that the awakening of the Kundalini will lead to encountering all one's blockages, that is, what C.G. Jung called the "shadow". If one should not already be completely healed, the Kundalini will first of all lead the one who tries to awaken Kundalini into the realm of the shadows …

In this connection it is of great importance, of course, how one is attuned to one's own shadow. Is it something that should be thrown out as soon as possible? Is it something that has to be ignored? Is it something that should be healed and integrated? Is it even the work of the devil?

In connection with the awakening of Kundalini it is helpful if one can see one's own shadow as the sum of undigested experiences and imprints from one's own past – then one can meet one's own shadow and transform it.

As long as one experiences the shadow as a disease or even as an enemy, the encounter with it is difficult. However, if one understands, for example, a fear as an attempt to survive or a pain as a warning of danger, the (re)encounter with these feelings becomes easier and one can heal them, transform them and direct the life force trapped in them in a new direction.

VI 3. Integration Method

This method, which is basically quite simple, I have partly developed myself, and I have had its basic features explained to me on dream journeys by my Kundalini.

This method consists of starting with simple Kundalini meditations to stimulate the Kundalini. You continue with this as long as you either experience the Kundalini and the chakras or as you become aware of your own blockages in meditation or in dreams. Then you look for these blockages and heal them.

If nothing happens in the meditation, one increases the meditation by adding new elements, prolonging it, doing it more often, etc.. Then one takes care of the newly appearing phenomena again. This gentle approach, in which one brings into consciousness only as much as one can "digest" well, leads to the fact that there are no great crises. Of course, the encounter with a trauma of which one was unaware can still be violent, but this approach is with some probability the most peaceful method of Kundalini awakening possible.

For dealing with the things one experiences when one gradually heats up "the fire under one's own butt" by one's meditations, my Kundalini has recommended the following method to me, which has proven very successful and which has also worked in every situation so far:

1. "look": You look at what you have encountered in your own inner feelings, memories, images and the like. Which feeling is that exactly? From which time in your life does this image originate? What was your role in the event at that time? Did this experience have consequences for your own behavior? Has the event repeated itself in a similar way? Which constellation does this correspond to in your own horoscope? Where do these feelings appear in your dreams? etc.

By this, little by little, a clearer and clearer picture of the things one has encountered in one's own inner life emerges.

In this process, one faces the feelings, images, etc. within oneself with a certain objective detachment.

2. "feel": In the second step, one gets involved, so to speak, with these feelings, images, etc. – one makes contact with them. It is important to "keep your head above water": If the feelings or images become too intense, one withdraws. By this gradual, step-by-step approach to these images and feelings, they gradually lose some of their terror and one can bear and endure more and more of them.

By the first step of "looking" you get an idea of what has arisen in you; by the second step of "feeling" you gradually become familiar with what you have encountered. In the process, the stress that lies in these images and feelings gradually relaxes.

During the first step, but at the latest during the second step, it also becomes clear to you from which time of your own life these feelings and images originate. Of course, one was younger then than now – and this younger self often appears as an inner figure. If this younger self does not appear of its own accord, it can be specifically sought or summoned.

This younger self is not identical with the feelings and images that the Kundalini has awakened – the younger self is the memory of oneself at the time when one experienced these images and feelings and when one obviously felt helpless and at least could not process the experiences of that time in an effective and efficient way.

3. "Embrace": This step is quite simple – you embrace your younger self. This sounds quite simple and unspectacular, but it has a great effect: the helpless younger self is integrated into the present self and thus finds support.

By "looking" one recognizes what one is dealing with; by "feeling" one makes contact with it; by "embracing" one integrates it. In this way a blockage is dissolved.

Of course, one cannot reduce the entire self-healing process to these three steps, but they are an extremely helpful and effective tool, which also has the great advantage of making all the processes gentle and reducing the dramas in self-healing to a very low level.

VI 4. Relaxation

It may sound strange that if one wants to achieve something, one should not exert oneself, but relax. Such a behavior only makes sense if there is a healed, right state from which one has deviated by cramps, avoidance postures, efforts, and the like. In this case, relaxation leads back to the healthy state.

The blockages at the intermediate chakras are such tense, rigid efforts that can lead to a sick state in the psyche and in the body.

Relaxation has two different effects, but they are interrelated.

> - On the one hand, relaxation causes one to turn one's attention away from the outside to the inside – bringing oneself closer to the realm of life force. This has already been briefly described at the very beginning of this book in the comparison of Kundalini, astral travel and hypnosis.
>
> By this inward view, one may also perceive one or the other blockage.

> - On the other hand, relaxation leads to the fact that one's own blockages loosen up a bit and become more visible and tangible.

There is a third relaxation effect that can be helpful in connection with the awakening of Kundalini:

> - When one relaxes and then feels the heaviness and warmth and the 6Hz-vibration of the body, that is, actually begins to feel one's own life force body, it also happens that one can perceive one of one's own chakras, or a flowing between them, or even the Kundalini itself.
>
> These can be the first glimpses of the Kundalini, which becomes much more tangible, which in turn can facilitate one's own Kundalini meditations – something that one has seen before ceases to be an abstract concept and becomes a concrete counterpart.

In what way one performs this relaxation is entirely up to one's own preference. In general, it will be beneficial to lie down. One can relax the individual limbs and organs in turn; one can relax in general; one can imagine floating in a warm sea; one can imagine being in the womb; one can do letter exercises; one can listen to music … there are, as almost always, many possibilities …

Relaxation is also a good basis for one-pointed and therefore relaxed concentration on the root chakra.

VI 5.   Physical Posture

Some things have already been said briefly about the physical posture during meditation. The best known in this context are the Indian asanas, but there are also other
systems that are extremely effective, such as the runic postures. If one stands in such
a posture and chants for an hour the mantras belonging to the rune in question, a lot
can happen. I myself have experienced the most intense rising of my Kundalini
during such a rune chanting.

The yoga asanas and the rune postures are not the only effective postures – in the
end, every posture leads to a particular chakra being emphasized and therefore
becoming more easily conscious. So you can also just try different postures and sing
an "a".

I myself, for example, experience my solar plexus most often when I am sitting at
my PC and concentrated on writing. Apparently the combination of sitting upright,
concentrating and being highly motivated is a good basis for awakening one's solar
plexus.

In an earlier chapter, the arrangement of the body parts on the cerebral cortex
("cortex") has been described. This arrangement is divided into four successive
sections:

    1. genitals
    2. toes – feet – legs – body (outside) – neck – head
    3. shoulders – arms – hands – fingers
    4. eyes – nose – lips – teeth – tongue – throat – intestines

If this arrangement should have any connection with the Kundalini, it would be
obvious to adopt a posture in Kundalini meditation in which the gaps in this arrangement are bridged. This results in the following posture:

    Kundalini is awakened in the root chakra, which is located at the genitals
    (section 1) – that fits well already.

    The jump from the genitals to the feet can be bridged by sitting on one's
    heels as in the Vir Asana ("Dragon") – then the root chakra is in contact with
    the feet.

    Then the Kundalini rises up to the crown chakra – which corresponds to the
    sequence in the second part of the arrangement of the body zones on the
    cortex of the cerebrum (section 2).
    In this context, one may ask what about the legs – but there is also the

possibility of awakening the Kundalini in the foot minor chakras – this will be described in more detail later in this book.

In the body zone arrangement in the Cortex, the head is followed by the arms from the shoulders to the fingers (section 3). They have no direct counterpart in Kundalini meditation at first.

However, since the rising current of Kundalini unfolds above the head into a "fountain" and then flows back down around the outside of the body, the arms from the shoulders to the hands would correspond to this downward movement.

How can you bridge the gap between the hands at the end of section 3 to the eyes at the beginning of section 4? The easiest way is to place the hands on the eyes. In the oldest Indian and Germanic representations of the Vir Asana, the meditators stretch their upper arms down to the sides and their lower arms up vertically, so that the hands are to the side of the head and near the face.

Now on the cortex follows the line from the eyes over the mouth and then inside further to the intestines (section 4). This obviously also corresponds to the downward flow of the life force outside around the body.

Section 4 ends with the viscera, which are then followed by section 1 with the genitals – so here the contact is already present.

In the cortex, these four sections form a circle – which corresponds to the convection current of the life force in the body.

The posture of the Vir Asana ("Dragon"), which has been classically used for the awakening of Kundalini, is obviously quite an exact correspondence to the arrangement of the body zones on the cortex of the cerebrum. This does not look like a coincidence.

To what extent during the awakening of Kundalini e.g. also a electrical current in the cortex occurs, has not been researched so far to my knowledge – but it would not be surprising if it were so.

However, one could not reduce the Kundalini to this current flow, because this electrical current would not explain e.g. why the Tibetan Lamas with their Kundalini meditation can dry their robes dipped in water in icy night.

This supposed electrical current would be a physical correspondence to the Kundalini, which is a process at the border between consciousness and matter/body and therefore has correspondences in the consciousness as well as in the body.

These reflections on this posture show above all that it is probably beneficial to also use the "dragon" as a meditation posture when awakening the Kundalini – either only this posture or together with others.

VI 6.   Dream Journeys

A dream journey is nothing exotic, but something quite common: If one wakes up from a dream in the morning and the dream continues for a few seconds in its own dynamics with oneself as a conscious spectator, this is a dream journey – even if a quite short one. However, one can reach the coordination of waking consciousness and dream consciousness (= subconsciousness) not only from a dream, but also from the waking consciousness: If you are sitting in the train and are bored and drift off into a daydream and relive your last vacation at the seaside and feel again the sun on your skin and the sand under your feet, that is also a dream journey.

You can get into this state, where you can consciously look at the inner images, on purpose with a little practice.

A great advantage of these dream journeys is that with their help you can explore your own inner self – including your own chakras and your own Kundalini.

A second advantage of dream journeys is that they provide easy access to telepathy, which is, so to speak, the sensory perception of the subconscious mind. Therefore, with the help of dream journeys it is possible to perceive things that cannot be perceived with the normal senses.

In connection with the awakening of Kundalini, one can use such dream journeys to get to know one's own fears, addictions, pains, etc., which become conscious by Kundalini meditation. This can be inner images, inner conversations with body parts, intuitive knowledge about some things – there are many different forms.

VI 7.   Conversations with Kundalini

If you have a little practice with dream journeys, you can also talk to your own Kundalini. You can just try it out: Inwardly address your own Kundalini and tell her that you want to get to know her, and then see what you see, hear, feel, etc.

At the beginning you can't know if what you perceive is not all just "fantasy" – but if you don't try it, you can never find out. In the end, there is only one criterion for the classification and evaluation of these "inner conversations": If they help you to get where you want to go, these conversations are useful – if they do not help you, they are not useful …

For myself, these conversations with my Kundalini have become one of the most important tools in the awakening of my Kundalini and in my self-healing.

Basically, this is obvious: talking to the part of yourself that you want to heal and awaken seems almost natural and indispensable.

VI 8. Classical Singing

Kundalini Awakening and Classical Singing would hardly be associated with each other as a rule. Nevertheless, Classical Singing can be used for the awakening of Kundalini.

Of course, the basics of classical singing cannot be presented in a short chapter – especially since there are quite different schools of singing. Of them, the "Lichtenberg Method" of classical singing has the greatest similarity with the "Integration Method" of Kundalini Meditation, which has already been presented.

The chanting exercise conducive to the awakening of Kundalini is quite simple:

- One stands upright, feet firmly on the ground, knees slightly bent (basic posture of Eastern martial techniques).

- One chants a vowel, e.g. an "a" at a pitch that is comfortable to oneself. It probably makes sense to do this for a while, playing with the breath, the length of the sound, the pitch, etc., until you find a comfortable way of singing.

- Then one adds an imagination: one imagines that one's own abdomen is filled with burning oil up to just below the navel. While singing, the flames blaze up to the throat and out of the mouth or further up to the crown of the head. This imagination is very powerful.

If you use this method more extensively, you can gradually discover the natural vibrato of your own voice (about 6Hz) and the variety of overtones – but this cannot be described well in a nutshell.

However, one approach of the Lichtenberg method is so valuable that it should be described here. It is so simple that at first it is not obvious that it should have an effect at all – as is often the case with basic methods …

One stands and sings a vowel, e.g. an "a", on a constant pitch. While doing so, one pays attention to whether the tone was rather soft, whether it was almost breathy ("toneless"), whether it was very short, whether one felt fear, whether the voice broke off, whether the voice became rough, etc.

Then you tell the breathlessness, the fear, the breathed voice or whatever you may have noticed that you are now lending it your own voice. So, for example, you offer the fear that it can now sing through your own voice. Thereby the fear can show itself and express itself – this corresponds to the "look" of the already presented method "look, feel, embrace".

So one sings again, i.e. the fear, to which one has made one's own voice available, sings through one's voice.

Now one pays attention to one's own voice again and is attentive to how it sounds. Then you make your own voice available again to what you notice in the process.

This method is, so to speak, a way of getting to know oneself with the help of one's own singing – this method is therefore roughly equivalent to dream journeys.

VI 9.   Homeopathy and Osteopathy

Kundalini helps to dissolve one's own blockages. It is therefore obvious to use other methods that can help in this healing.

Homeopathy is a good choice, because it always looks at the whole person and chooses the right remedy for him. Homeopathy does not "take away" a disease, but brings the whole person back into balance. If you have found a good homeopath who can choose the right "constitutional remedy" for you, this can be a great help in awakening the Kundalini.

A second option is to seek help from an osteopath. These doctors are, so to speak, the "precision mechanics of the body", who can recognize and treat misalignments of joints, spasms of muscles, shortening of tendons, and more. Since the states of the body result from the states of the psyche, it can be a great help if the body as a whole is again in a "healthy posture". This, of course, does not obviate the need to dissolve the mental blockages, but if there is no longer a corresponding physical blockage attached to the mental blockage, one has to move less overall to return to the healed state …

VI 10. Herbs and Drugs

People have always tended to look for technical shortcuts to inner processes, ranging from initiation rituals to extreme physical exercises to drugs.

Most herbs and drugs have the great disadvantage that they either do not have much effect or that they lead to death if taken in the wrong dosage. This danger is due to the fact that astral projection and Kundalini fire are quite evident in a near-death experience – so in drug-induced near-death you experience astral projection and Kundalini.

Therefore, drugs are either not very effective or very dangerous. The safest way to use them is still in a traditional setting, where the leader knows the substances used very well, can judge well the person who wants to take them, and can also guide him or her.

This does not mean, of course, that one cannot be successful alone in experiments with herbs, mushrooms and the like. But it is quite dangerous and can end in death or permanent damage to the psyche if the wrong dosage is used.

Another argument against drugs is that all the experiences one can have under drugs can also be achieved without drugs by the appropriate meditations, dream rituals, rituals, etc. In this way one avoids fatal wrong doses and thus also fatal consequences – and as a rule one will only experience as much as one can process by meditative and ritualistic methods. In addition, one does not become dependent on the availability of drugs.

But in the end, of course, everyone has to decide for himself which way suits him and which way he wants to go …

VI 11. Dance

If the Kundalini is hindered by blockages, then everything that brings movement should be beneficial … Therefore, dancing and especially fully improvised dancing is something that can loosen up these blockages and that can help one to remember what it is like when one can flow more freely again instead of just having to act rigidly.

One should not underestimate the effect of dance improvisation, even if at first glance it does not seem to have much to do with Kundalini.

I did not find music that fitted my ideas about a Kundalini dance. So I composed one myself: a rising of the Kundalini up through the seven chakras. It's 48 minutes long and may be found at youtube: „Harry Eilenstein – The chakra Dance of Kundalini".

VI 12.   Ecstasy

"Ecstasy" is a colorful term, but basically ecstasy is something quite simple: one-pointedness. The pathological variant is fixation, i.e. the rigid orientation e.g. to a drug, a relationship, power, fame, etc. Ecstasy is best known in the context of sexuality as orgasm.

One can use different tools to reach the state of ecstasy. The most important is, of course, the motivation, that is, the desire to reach a certain state – or even better, to achieve something specific with the help of this ecstasy.

Among the various signs of the zodiac, Scorpio generally seems to find it easiest to reach the state of ecstasy. This is because they tend to be one-pointed – the planet Pluto belongs to Scorpio and Pluto embodies the existential and therefore the one-pointed. But ecstasy, of course, is available to everyone.

 One-pointedness to one's root chakra is an effective way to awaken Kundalini. Therefore, it is worthwhile to take a closer look at the different methods of ecstasy.

Basically, it is enough to sit quietly and concentrate completely and without wavering on one's own root chakra. However, since this is not easy for everyone, some tools for this concentration have been developed over the millennia. Ultimately, both meditation and ecstasy strive for unity – but while meditation becomes more and more silent and motionless, ecstasy becomes more and more loud and moving, so to speak.

This loudness and these movements are on the one hand rhythmic and on the other hand directed towards the goal – they help one to "get into" something.

> - A simple form is the singing of a mantra or a short song verse, which is constantly repeated. Chanting together is a great support: if everyone focuses on the same thing (e.g. Shiva) and chants the same thing, it coordinates the psyches and the life force bodies of the participants, which then begin to vibrate together – which then carries the individual and prevents him from digressing.

> - The second "classical" method besides singing is drumming. One beats a rhythm, carries the rhythm, is carried by the rhythm, becomes completely absorbed in the rhythm – and identifies the rhythm with one's own goal. This rhythm can either remain the same all the time or gradually increase – by increasing tempo, by increasing volume, by changing the pattern of beating, etc.

> Almost all shamans use a frame drum (tambourine, bodhran) for this purpose, which is the oldest form of drum (a skin stretched on a frame for tanning). This drum is often referred to as the horse for the shamans' journeys

into the otherworld.

The drumming is often, but not always, accompanied by the chanting of the shaman or a group of helpers.

- The third "classical" method is dance. This is usually accompanied by drumming and usually also singing – although the dancers themselves only occasionally sing along.

When dancing, one moves with the rhythm of the drumming. This causes the entire body to vibrate and become filled with the theme to which the singing, drumming and dancing refer.

A typical element of ecstasy dances is the stomping of the feet, which is very characteristic of African dances. This movement grounds, concentrates, brings to the ground, gathers strength, connects with the earth – the best way to understand this is to try it once. With each stomp, you summon what you want to achieve. This element also exists in a weakened form in the purely rhythmic parts of Indian temple dance ("Kathakali").

A second element is the pantomimic representation, in which often disguises and masks are used. Usually this pantomime creates the framework in which the purely rhythmic part then takes place: The pantomime describes and summons the deity, into which the dancer in question then enters by a purely rhythmic dance. This "division of tasks" is also found in traditional African dances.

There are also special forms of ecstasy dance such as the dervish dances. In them, the dancers turn in a circle for a long time and look into their outstretched hand, which they hold in front of them with the palm facing them. The trick is simple: as long as you look at the palm, you can keep spinning – but as soon as you look into your surroundings, the spinning makes you dizzy and nauseous. This dance virtually forces the dancer to become one-pointed, or else he will become nauseous.

This is basically the same sly tactic as that of the Tibetan lamas who had their disciples practice Kundalini meditation by having their disciples drying wet clothes on their bodies in freezing cold. The unpleasant circumstances that occur when one leaves one-pointedness (nausea, cold) facilitate one-pointedness.

This tactic is also found in fire walking, where one walks barefoot over glowing coals.

Ecstasy dances are usually danced over a longer period of time – a good time is at least half an hour at a stretch, better a whole hour. This is also true for drumming and singing. With practice, of course, the time it takes to get into one-pointedness by dancing can become much shorter.

If one performs such dances but is not in tune, they are extremely tiring and one is quite exhausted afterwards. However, if you perform a war dance, for example, and you are actually angry at someone and declare war on them and dance, you gain strength from the dance – the movements no longer have to be consciously controlled, but arise of their own accord out of the motivation: the dance begins to flow out of your own center and is one-pointed and full of power.

- A special form of the ecstasy technique is sexuality. It will be discussed in the following chapter ("Tantra").

- A basis of many ecstasy methods is the identification with a deity ("invocation"). The method depends, of course, on the character of the chosen deity – although most ecstasy rituals will also include an invocation to the deity and possibly chanted mantras and songs to that deity.

These invocations may look very different: In an invocation to Pan, one will play and dance on the pan flute; in an invocation to Krishna, one will play and dance on the transverse flute; to Apollo, the lyre fits; to Dagda and Bragi, the harp; to the West African thunder god Shango, the drum; in an invocation to Osiris, the world tree ("Djed") plays an important role; in an invocation to the earth and otherworld goddesses, the sweat lodge or the burial mound may be important, etc.

It is not absolutely necessary to practice a method of dance ecstasy to awaken the Kundalini, but it might be worthwhile to try an impromptu Kundalini dance and call the Kundalini up from the earth and into oneself, singing and stomping.

VI 13. Tantra

"Tantra" means "fabric" and originally refers to the summary and expansion of the original scriptures of Buddhism called "sutra", i.e. "threads".

There have been three stages in Buddhism:

> 1. The <u>Hinayana</u> ("little way"), which is the oldest method that seeks to change one's situation by right conduct – it is roughly equivalent to the Old Testament.

> 2. The <u>Mahayana</u> ("great way"), which places charity at the center of one's efforts – this method corresponds roughly to the New Testament

> 3. The <u>Vajrayana</u> ("diamond way"), which is the youngest method and uses various methods to reach enlightenment as quickly as possible – it corresponds roughly to the Christian mystics

"Tantra", then, actually refers to the direction of Buddhism in which one is very committed, willing to take risks, and is single-mindedly striving for enlightenment in this very life.

> One of the many methods used for this is sexuality. This use is based on the fact that sexuality is one of the greatest driving forces in human beings. The method, which is mostly called "Tantra Yoga" in the West today, consists of a man and a woman uniting, but not allowing an orgasm. One moves only enough to maintain the tension, and feels inside oneself what is happening there. This may sound boring, but you can experience many things this way.

> A second aspect of this method is that one carries within oneself the image of the healed man and the healed woman. One can understand these two images as the polar mirror images of one's own soul in the life force. One can find these two inner images by meditations, dream journeys and rituals. To get to one's soul, it is often necessary to unite the inner man and the inner woman.

In yoga, the inner man and woman are associated with the two minor life force channels, Ida and Pingala. In order to become fully oneself, it is necessary to direct the life force located in Ida and Pingala to the Sushumna, that is, to the main life force channel in the middle. This corresponds to the union of the inner man with the inner woman, which can either be imagined in a meditation or ritually performed with a concrete partner. The sushumna is connected with one's own soul. This yoga method mainly uses pranayama, i.e. breath control.

Since the psyche does not only consist of the soul as its seed and of its two whole, polar mirror images, i.e. of the inner man and the inner woman, but becomes more and more complex in the course of life by the most diverse experiences, some distorted images of women and men in the psyche arise from the two whole images. These distorted inner images shape the psyche and one's behavior to a very great extent.

Altogether, the image of the soul, the whole inner images of women and men, and the distorted images of women and men in one's psyche are an inner mandala.

The distorted images of women and men in one's own psyche correspond to the three pathological polarizations already presented, which also correspond to the three pairs of chakras: addict and ascetic, perpetrator and victim, and star and fan.

I have described this mandala, its origin, its structure and its healing by a mandala ritual in detail in "Das Beziehungs-Mandala".

Of course, in order to awaken the Kundalini, one does not need to know this inner mandala, but it can be very helpful in orientation and in recognizing the next sensible step.

A simple meditation based on this inner man/woman mandala will be described in more detail in a later chapter.

VI 14. Teacher

It is a question of style whether to seek a teacher or not. Some people need this form of support and guidance – for others, however, such a teacher is only an obstacle. Everyone has to find out what works for him by himself.

The advantage of a good teacher is, of course, that he knows and has mastered what you are looking for yourself. In this respect, a teacher can be a shortcut, a pathfinder, a bridge over an abyss …

If it suits you to learn from a teacher, and if you have a clear and definite motivation, you will find the right teacher. If the motivation is unclear, the teacher will also be unclear … one finds what suits one, i.e. what reflects one's inner self most accurately …

VI 15.   Self-Fidelity

The basis of all these methods is the striving for what one wants – or for rightness, salvation … however one wants to describe the desired state.

The Kundalini is the tool, an aid, a healer – the free flowing Kundalini is the best possible state.

This aspiration has self-fidelity as its foundation.

VI 16.   Here and Now

Resting in the here and now is also an important point. Where could one concentrate, where could one experience, and where could one do something if not in the here and now? The here and now belongs to one-pointedness – only in the here and now can one be completely "with it".

Therefore, the question "What do I want exactly here and now?" is important again and again. If one merely asks oneself this question again and again and so often that one begins to become completely present in the present, one will reach a completely new state … the Kundalini, too, can only flow freely in the here and now …

VII   The Ignition of Kundalini

In all this, the question naturally arises as to how the flow of Kundalini can be set in motion, how the fire of Kundalini can be ignited, how its flight into the heights can be stimulated, how its flourishing can be brought about. How and where does this process begin?

As with almost everything, there are once again several possibilities.

VII 1.   Root Chakra

The best known case is certainly the ignition of Kundalini in the root chakra. This seems to be the main method in India. Probably this is also the oldest method, since it is known by the Indians as well as by the Germanic tribes and therefore it can be traced back to the Indogermanics. This method is also known from the Tibetans, who adopted it from the Indians. Otherwise, there seems to be very sparse concrete evidence as to which chakra one awakens the Kundalini in.

As a rule, the Kundalini is led up from the root chakra to the crown chakra – some instructions, however, recommend to lead the Kundalini afterwards back from the crown chakra to the third eye, by which this power can be directed and used in magic.

VII 2.   Solar Plexus

The ignition of Kundalini in the solar plexus is found mainly in Tibet. It seems that it is easiest to feel the life force in the solar plexus – which may have inspired the Tibetans to experiment with igniting Kundalini in the solar plexus.

The awakening and rising of Kundalini from the solar plexus sometimes also occurs spontaneously – so it seems to be a natural process.

In this case, too, the Kundalini is usually led up to the crown chakra.

VII 3.   Foot Chakras

A third possibility is the ignition of Kundalini in the foot chakras. This is mainly known as the "Weinfurter Method". In this method, one imagines one of the five vowels in the middle of the soles of one's feet for a few minutes at a time, chanting them inwardly. One thus directs one's own concentration to the minor chakras in one's feet.

In this case, the heat awakens in the feet and then rises up through the legs to the root chakra, and from there it continues up the usual path.

VII 4.   Head

The last possibility is to ignite Kundalini in the head, i.e. in the third eye. This possibility, like the previous method, is rather unknown. It is called "Sebottendorf method" or "Sebottendorf letter exercises". It consists of some words and gestures that are performed regularly. In this method, the life force is led from the third eye down to the navel.

However, this method has a tendency to awaken one's shadows in a somewhat chaotic manner, so it is not really recommended.

VII 5. Summary

It is interesting to note where the Kundalini can be ignited. If you look at the arrangement of the body zones in the cerebrum cortex, you will find some similarities. This arrangement is:

1. genitals
2. toes – feet – legs – body (outside) – neck – head
3. shoulders – arms – hands – fingers
4. eyes – nose – lips – teeth – tongue – throat – intestines

The classical awakening of Kundalini corresponds to section 1: in the genitalia located at the root chakra, and then upward in section 2.

The awakening of Kundalini according to the Weinfurt Method corresponds to section 2: from the feet and the foot chakras upwards.

The awakening of the Kundalini in the solar plexus starts in the middle of section 2.

The awakening of Kundalini in the Sebottendorf method corresponds to section 4: from the eyes and the third eye downwards to the navel.

It seems that no one has ever tried to ignite the Kundalini in the shoulders and then direct it down to the hands. This would be something that could possibly be expected from spiritual healers and the like who direct the life force with their hands.

The genitals, i.e. the root chakra is located at the beginning of the body zones on the cortex and is therefore apparently also the natural starting point for the awakening of Kundalini. The feet (foot chakras) and the eyes (third eye) are also located at the beginning of a section and therefore are also suitable for igniting the Kundalini. However, as the ignition of Kundalini in the solar plexus shows, the awakening of Kundalini is not limited to these three points in the body (plus the shoulders?).

VIII   The Experience of Kundalini

What does the Kundalini feel like when it is awakened? These perceptions are closely related to the experiences in the seven main chakras and also to the experience of blockages in these chakras.

Fortunately, the perception of the life force in the chakras seems to be quite uniform, so that for once we can describe something that is more or less universal.

VIII 1.   Life Force Experiences in the Chakras

The experience of life force in the chakras is just as different as the various functions of the chakras.

VIII 1. a)   Root Chakra

In the root chakra, the life force is most often experienced as a spinning and glowing – which may have contributed a good part to the fire serpent symbolism. This spinning has a frequency of about 0.5Hz – so one spin takes about 2 seconds.

However, there are still some variations to this perception such as a sort of "light, cool heat" – this is a paradoxical description, but captures the perception quite well. There is also something effortless, simple and natural about this sensation.

The sensation that often occurs first is a light, pleasant, pulsating pressure that gives the impression of "awakening vitality".

These perceptions may gradually increase to a more and more intense heat.

VIII 1. b)   Hara

The sensation in the hara is rather unspectacular: it feels like a light warm pressure that conveys support and inner peace and steadfastness.

VIII 1. c) Solar Plexus

The sensation in the solar plexus is very distinctive: a "glittering, electric tingling" that after a while spreads out in all directions like veins.

Sometimes there is also a feeling of pressure, slight burning and discomfort, which at first is not easily distinguishable from great hunger.

The solar plexus may also begin to "burn", which is a sensation that is grasped, but at the same time very lively and alive.

When the solar plexus properly "ignites," there is an intense heat that is directed upward in the form of a ray or a tube. You usually start to sweat at this point.

VIII 1. d) Heart Chakra

The sensation of the awakening heart chakra sounds decidedly corny, but it is like that: a love-filled glow. The whole chest area is filled with warmth, love and happiness, although this love does not refer to anyone specifically and this happiness has no cause. Warmth, love and happiness are what is contained in the heart chakra and what the heart chakra radiates – nothing is needed to get into this state, only something is sought by which to express these feelings.

This feeling is probably what is commonly described as "I feel so warm around my heart."

This feeling is one of the most fulfilling things one can experience – it ends all lack, fear and self-doubt and is the root of fullness, power and self-love.

VIII 1. e) Throat Chakra

The throat chakra, like actually every chakra, is initially felt as a slight pressure.

However, this pressure can increase to a radiance and a feeling of sovereigty and freedom and uninhibited social self-expression.

VIII 1. f) Third Eye

In the Third Eye there is at first a quiet stirring, a presence that feels almost like a light touch.

This then gradually becomes a pulsating pressure, and this pulsation may become very distinct. This pulsation has a frequency of about 1Hz, or one pulsation per second.

This sensation is associated with a feeling of clarity, alignment, determination and direction.

VIII 1. g) Crown Chakra

Sometimes one first notices something like a ring around the head, running from the base of the skull, over the ears and at the hairline at the top of the forehead. This ring is also known as the "migraine ring" because in migraine the pain occurs preferentially there. If you wear a crown, it will sit on this ring – thus "crown chakra".

This ring-pressure sensation may be joined by a "radiating upward" sensation, possibly associated with a slight tingling sensation.

In the next stage, this tingling sensation fills the whole upper head above the "migraine ring".

Next, the entire crown, or top of the head, then seems to bulge upward – this has led to the image of Buddha with the topknot on his head. In this arched-up part of the head, there is a feeling of a bright radiance.

VIII 1. h) Hand Chakras

In the hand chakras, the first sensation is a slight pressure, then a pulsation at about 0.5Hz, and finally a rotation at 0.5Hz (one revolution in 2 seconds). There is the sensation that the hand chakras either emit life force or absorb life force.

VIII 1. i) Foot Chakras

In the soles of the feet, the activity of the chakras there can be felt as a light, pleasant pressure connecting with the earth. Presumably, the same pulsation and rotation may occur there as in the hand chakras.

VIII 2.   The Experience of Kundalini

The Kundalini awakens with a sequence of several sensations – it is unlikely that this is exactly the same for all people, but this sequence seems to be quite common.

VIII 2. a)   Electric Tingling

The first stage is a slight electric tingle, quite similar to the sensation in the awakening of the solar plexus. This sensation becomes interesting, invigorating and makes one curious for more.

VIII 2. b)   Heat

The second stage of sensation is an airy, flying heat that envelops the whole body – though usually not the legs and arms and sometimes not the head. This heat moves shimmeringly like the air in hot summer on an asphalt road. This heat is unsteady and constantly flies with its center of intensity from one body zone to another like a streak of mist.

VIII 2. c)   Heat Envelope

Next, a heat envelope is formed, whereby this is usually connected with a relaxed, "soft" concentration, which happens "as if by the way", so to speak. Presumably, it is this warmth envelope that Tibetan monks use to keep warm in winter.

This warmth envelope is associated with the feeling of fullness and contentment as well as relaxation.

VIII 2. d)   Glow

Finally, the concentrated, tubular glow occurs. This "glow tube" grows gradually from the bottom upward – with the "speed of a crawling turtle," as the Indian scriptures put it. From the root chakra to the crown chakra this is about 40-50 seconds.

However, there is also the variant in which the Kundalini heat shoots up very suddenly.

VIII 2. e)   The Kundalini Outside the Body

After rising, the Kundalini continues to move upward beyond the crown, then flows back down and gathers again in the root chakra. This can be experienced as a great expansion of consciousness.

VIII 2. f)   Serpent Vision

The rising heat can sometimes be experienced and seen inwardly as a snake or a dragon. The movement of Kundalini in the central Sushumna and also in Ida and Pingala next to it sometimes appears like a silvery-grey shining tube, which becomes longer and longer towards the top and grows upwards. The resemblance of this perception to a crawling snake coming out of the root chakra is very great, even though usually no head is visible at the upper end of the snake.

VIII 3.   Experience of Blockages

The blockages in the life force flow may be experienced in quite different ways: as pressure, as hardening ("stone"), as almost physical pain (usually a twinge) and various others.

These blockages are usually located at the intermediate chakras, i.e. at the base of the pubic hair, at the navel, at the lower end of the anterior sternum, at the upper end of the anterior sternum, at the palate and at the hairline on the forehead ("migraine ring"). This prevents the flow of life force between the two main chakras above and below this "closed gate" – which can also lead to unpleasant sensations in the main chakra itself.

VIII 3. a)   Main Blockage and Opposite Pole

As a rule, there is a main blockade, which is characterized by the fact that almost all life force is dammed up in the chakra that one uses for survival. This means that the intermediate chakra on the side of this main chakra facing the heart chakra is blocked: it jams the life force in this main chakra.

The opposite chakra to the chakra with the life force congestion is in life force deficiency – the intermediate chakra on the heart side of this main chakra is also blocked: It does not let any life force into this main chakra.

The six standard possibilities for such a dual blockage are:

      1. a) <u>Addict</u> (greed).
          - life force congestion in the root chakra
            due to a blockage in the pubic intermediate chakra
              and
          - life force deficiency in the crown chakra
            by a blockage in the main hair intermediary chakra

      1. b) <u>Asceticism</u> (renunciation)
          - life force congestion in the crown chakra
             due to a blockage in the main hair intermediate chakra
              and
          - life force deficiency in the root chakra
             due to a blockage in the pubic intermediary chakra

2. a) <u>Perpetrator</u> (power)
  - life force congestion in the hara
    due to a blockage in the umbilical intermediary chakra
      and
  - life force deficiency in the third eye
    due to a blockage in the palatal intermediary chakra

2. b) Victim (powerlessness)
  - life force congestion in the third eye
    due to a blockage in the palatal intermediary chakra
      and
  - life force deficiency in the hara
    due to a blockage in the umbilical intermediary chakra

3. a) <u>Star</u> (delusion of grandeur)
  - life force congestion in the solar plexus
    due to a blockage in the wish tree intermediate chakra
      and
  - life force deficiency in the throat chakra
    due to a blockage in the thymus intermediate chakra

3. b) <u>Fan</u> (inferiority complex)
  - life force congestion in the throat chakra
    due to a blockage in the thymus intermediate chakra
      and
  - life force deficiency in the solar plexus
    due to a blockage in the wish tree intermediate chakra

There is an interesting dynamic here: every addict attracts an ascetic – and vice versa; every perpetrator attracts a victim – and vice versa; and every star attracts a fan – and vice versa.

This means that the awakening of Kundalini and the healing of one's psyche that accompanies it also has a social component: One must confront the antithesis of one's own behavior. Only in this way one may find one's way back to the healed state: addict and ascetic to abundance; perpetrator and victim to strength; and star and fan to self-love.

This confrontation with one's own antipole on the outside is often anything but a pleasure, but this "tormentor" is the one who makes it unmistakably clear to oneself where one's own unhealed wounds and thus one's own unresolved blockages lie.

VIII 3. b)   Six Ways of Healing

As we have just seen, one usually has a main blockage (life force congestion), which is supplemented by the blockage in the other chakra belonging to this pair (life force deficiency).

Each of these six possible forms of blockage of the life force has, over the millennia, developed a way to use its own one-sidedness to heal itself: The addict uses improvisation, the ascetic uses austerity, the perpetrator uses determination, the victim uses devotion, the star uses the expansion of his self-esteem, and the fan uses devotion to a deity.

These six ways were once described to me by my Kundalini on a dream journey with the following verses:

> *The ascetic uses his rigidity,*
> *in order to bring the water of life through dams*
> *back into the original riverbed.*

> *The addict uses the improvised dance,*
> *to regain a sense*
> *for the momentum of the water of life.*

> *The victim seeks the ritual initiation death,*
> *to return to the heart of life.*

> *The perpetrator uses his power*
> *to face all inner fears*
> *and to rediscover his inner source behind them.*

> *The fan worships a deity*
> *and surrenders to it*
> *and returns to himself by bhakti-yoga.*

> *The star expands*
> *and finally sees himself as a god*
> *and thereby finds the source of life again.*

This kind of method has been developed by the indian Mahasiddhas about 1000 years ago. It was named „to get rid of water in the ear by water".

VIII 3. c)   The Three Granthis

In Yoga, the three Granthis are the three main obstacles on the path of the Kundalini from the root chakra up to the crown chakra.

> 1. the Rudra granthi in the third eye: With this blockage it helps to sit in the "dragon" (shins on the floor, buttocks on the heels) and to chant a bright "I" – thereby seeing things again as they really are. Rudra is a manifestation of Shiva.
> The Rudra granthi apparently blocks access to the strength and clarity that is the essence of the anal stage in human development.

> 2. the Vishnu-Granthi in the heart chakra: With this blockage it helps to arch the chest forward and chant a full "A" – thus sincerity may be recovered.
> The Vishnu granthi apparently blocks access to self-love, which is the essence of the phallic phase in human development.

> 3. the Brahma-Granthi in the root chakra: With this blockage it helps to sway the body back and forth, to chant a deep "U" – thereby security and fullness in life may arise again.
> The Brahma granthi apparently blocks access to security, which is the essence of the oral phase in human development.

Security (oral phase, Brahma), strength (anal phase, Shiva) and self-love (phallic phase, Vishnu) are the three foundations on which the psyche of man is built.

Probably the classical Indian chakra-assignments can be extended a little bit:

> - The assignment of Vishnu and self-love to the heart chakra is conclusive, since the heart chakra contains one's own identity. However, one should actually expect an assignment to the solar plexus and the throat chakra here, since these are the two chakras of self-expression and self-love (phallic phase) – they are located directly above and below the heart chakra, respectively.

> - The assignment of the Shiva and strength to the third eye is conclusive, since this chakra corresponds to the anal phase. The opposite pole to the third eye is the hara, which is the second strength chakra.

> - The assignment of Brahma and security to the root chakra is conclusive, since the root chakra corresponds to the oral phase. The opposite pole to the

root chakra is the crown chakra, which is the second security chakra.

Thus, the three granthis essentially correspond to the six possible blockages described in the previous two sections of this chapter.

VIII 3. d)   Reincarnation Trauma

One can take the consideration of blockages a little further and include past lives. However, this is not absolutely necessary, since one seems to restage all the karma one brings with oneself into this life during the first three years and thereby firmly anchors it in one's present life.

Therefore, the healing of all blockages in this life is sufficient – in doing so, one will heal the possible roots of these blockages in previous lives as well.

IX Meditations

After these considerations, one can now see how best to proceed in meditation. Of course, this cannot be determined in a general concrete way – it can only be said what one could try in which situation.

IX 1. Individual

If you are not the type who likes to follow a set plan or a teacher, you have to try things out – try them out, observe the effect, compare them with other methods, design and try a new method or a new combination of methods, talk to others about their experiences … In this way you will find your own way and acquire a solid expertise.

IX 1. a) Motivation

Motivation is the foundation of the whole – it determines what one strives for, which methods one chooses, how much time and energy one puts into one's experiments … Therefore it is useful to examine one's own motivation and to formulate one's own goals as accurately as possible.

From time to time you should check your motivation – maybe something has changed in it, because you have achieved some things, discovered some new possibilities, found some more methods, etc. Only by regularly reviewing the goal and the methods can one stay on the right course.

IX 1. b) One's Own Style

No matter what others say, it is important to be true to one's own style – no matter what that style may be. Some want to be guided, others want to explore on their own, some need great support and clear guidance, others build their practices on the teaching and power transmission of a teacher … Only by using one's own style one will truly succeed and be effective.

IX 2. Mantra

The vast majority of meditations use a mantra. Even in Kundalini meditations a mantra is mostly used. If there is no reason to use a specific, concrete mantra, the mantra "fire" is the most obvious, because most perceptions of the Kundalini and the chakras are forms of heat.

One can also experiment with different mantras, but it is better to commit oneself to one mantra for a longer time, because its effect will be greater.

IX 3. Breath

As described earlier, sometimes the mantra is accompanied by a certain breathing technique. In this case, the mantra is usually only spoken internally, since speaking is closely related to breath and therefore also shapes the rhythm of the breath.

Again, one should not change the method used too often.

IX 4. Posture

The posture is more variable than the mantra or the breathing rhythm. One can try different postures to see how they feel. If a posture is convincing, one can change to it and meditate, for example, no longer in the lotus position as before, but in the dragon.

But here, too, frequent changes are rather disturbing.

IX 5. Imaginations

There is a great variety of imaginations. Here, too, it is advisable to use one imagination as a basis and to keep it as a common thread in all variations. Around it, however, one can try out everything possible and see what the effect is.

IX 5. a)   Root Chakra

The root chakra will usually be the place in the body where one tries to awaken the Kundalini. The two alternatives that can be encountered more often are the solar plexus and the foot chakras. One can also experiment here, but one should also use one chakra as a continuous thread.

IX 5. b)   Sushumna

The yogi Naropa, who lived 1000 years ago and from whom today's Buddhist tradition in Tibet derives, recommended some preliminary exercises for the actual awakening of Kundalini. The most important of these is related to the sushumna.

> One imagines a tube in the middle of the body from the root chakra up to the crown chakra.
> Then one narrows this tube until the opening in it is only as big as the thickness of a hair.
> Then one widens this tube until the opening in it can hold the whole earth.
> One alternates back and forth between these two images several times.
> This is to make the sushumna elastic and permeable.

One can also imagine the sushumna as a rod of light in one's own body. This imagination, which Nropa showed me on a dream journey, is also very effective when one is confused, has turbulent feelings, or has otherwise lost one's footing.

IX 5. c)   Ida and Pingala

In these two life force channels adjacent to the sushumna, all three of which intersect at each chakra, lie the inner whole female image and the inner whole male image.

They play a major role in pranayama yoga, that is, in directing the breath through the body. According to the pranayama system, they end in the right and left nostrils – but I have often experienced that the life force has risen through these channels at least to the third eye, sometimes even further to the crown chakra.

Concentrating on these two life force channels can lead to experiencing them like two ascending snakes, which have a distinct momentum of their own and also an shape that appears by itself and does not need to be imagined – as already said two

73

silver-grey "tubes" that look like (headless) snakes and also move like them.

This rising of the life force in Ida and Pingala leads to the awakening of the crown chakra and to a greater self-stabilizing concentration.

IX 5. d) Three Nadis

The life force channels are collectively called "nadis" in India – the most important of which are Sushumna and Ida and Pingala.

The most important process in them is the directing of the life force from Ida and Pingala into Sushumna in the center. This corresponds to the realization that the whole inner man and woman (Ida and Pingala) are mirror images of one's own soul (Sushumna).

It seems to me that this directing of the life force to the center can also be stimulated by breathing exercises, but that it is a gentler and more organic method to direct the life force into Ida and Pingala and thereby stimulate them, if you just get to know them (e.g. by dream journeys), to find the images in them and to heal them – whereupon the focus then shifts by itself to the Sushumna, i.e. to one's own soul in the heart chakra.

But this is only my opinion, my approach and my style.

IX 5. e) Inner Man and Inner Woman

One can also stimulate the process of the union of Ida and Pingala to the Sushumna or the conducting of the life force from the two outer Nadis into the middle Nadi by imagination.

> To do this, one imagines the inner whole man sitting in the lotus posture on the root chakra, which one imagines as a lotus blossom. In front of him sits the inner whole woman.
>
> Both are naked. Both are looking at each other. When one feels that it is the right time, the woman sits down on the man's lap and both unite.
>
> Then you take your time and feel into this union.
>
> This process is repeated in the hara, solar plexus, heart chakra, throat chakra, third eye and crown chakra.

74

This meditation can be extended by visualizing the qualities and functions of each chakra and imagining that the man and woman uniting in it will restore the healing state of that chakra.

This imagination can be expanded further on in many ways: by talking to the two, by starting to sing inwardly to the respective chakra and the two in it, by letting oneself be filled with the quality of the union, by using the classical Indian chakra mantras, etc. Here it is beneficial to become creative according to one's own style.

IX 5. f) Sun Child

The image of one's own soul in the heart chakra, which is also associated with the Sushumna, may appear as a "sun child" – a radiant, happy, playing child. This archetype is also depicted, for example, on the Tarot card "The Sun".

You can call this archetype to you e.g. on a dream journey or invite it to appear to you after the union of the inner man with the inner woman described in the previous section. One can also undertake a dream journey into the sushumna or into the heart chakra in order to find one's own sun child – that is, to see oneself in the original, whole state.

Once one has found this sun child within oneself, the actual creative part that follows the healing begins: expressing who one is.

Of course, you are not completely healed immediately when you find your inner sun child, but you will know then who you actually are and what you want and how you want to live – that is a great help in healing.

The sun child is, so to speak, the collective image for the soul, the primordial soul image. You have to find the individual form of your own soul yourself – it is, of course, a little different for everyone.

IX 5. g) Fire

The imagination of fire in the root chakra is probably the most important single method for awakening Kundalini. Very often an equilateral red triangle or a pointed red triangle is imagined in the root chakra.

If this triangle is made to rotate around its vertical central axis, the triangle becomes a cone – which in my experience is a more effective imagination.

One can also use a red tetrahedron, that is, a Platonic solid whose surface consists of four equilateral triangles. This has the effect that from the upward pointing tip of

75

the tetrahedron the Sushumna spontaneously rises upward. Sometimes, in answer to this imagination, an inverted, i.e. with its tip pointing downwards, white tetrahedron is also spontaneously formed in the crown chakra. This creates an inner calm and stability.

IX 5. h) Slurping

There is a nowadays more widely known method of conducting the life force upward from the root chakra to the crown chakra. Since this method exerts some pressure on the life force, one should not use it too often at first and make sure that one takes the time to process and integrate the experiences that occur in the process.

The method, which is performed while sitting, is as follows:

- inhaling:
  - inhale the air with a clearly audible slurping sound
  - bend the pelvis forward
  - tense the pelvic floor muscles
  - imagine the rising of the life force as a white light.

- exhaling:
  - exhale the air in a clearly audible jerky manner
  - bend the pelvis backwards
  - relax the pelvic floor muscles
  - let go of the imagination

(The pelvis floor muscles are also called "pubococcygeus muscle". They are between the genitals and the anus. These are the muscles that are trained after childbirth.)

This exercise has similarities with Naropa's preliminary exercise of imagining the sushumna.

This exercise may cause one to feel the root chakra, feel heat in the head, see one's sushumna, etc. One should take time to contemplate and feel into these phenomena.

A relaxed approach is more effective in this exercise than dogged concentration – which, of course, ultimately applies to all activities related to the life force.

IX 5. i) Root Chakra of the Earth

The life-force body of man is not isolated – there is life-force in all things: in all men, animals, plants, stones, mountains, rivers, houses, machines, clouds, winds, stars, etc. – in fact, in everything. Therefore, all things have chakras and a life force flow.

Thus, it can be beneficial to connect one's root chakra to, for example, the the most intense place of life force of the earth, i.e. its glowing iron/nickel core. This is quite simple and quite effective.

> You send a ray of light from your root chakra down into the center of the earth while sitting, standing or lying down until you come to the glowing earth core.
>
> There one calls upon one's own share of this great power in the center of the earth. In most cases a snake or a dragon appears.
>
> This snake or dragon is then invoked into one's own body, whereupon it will rise, reach the root chakra and then fill one's own body.
>
> Sometimes this life force simply takes the form of a ray of light or a "long cloud of light".

This exercise increases one's own life force, strengthens, makes one more alive – although the effect is certainly a little different for each person.

IX 5. j) Light of Heaven

The same as for the root chakra applies also to the crown chakra – one can connect it with the sky.

> To do this, one sends a ray of light upward from the crown chakra and asks the light of heaven to flow down.

There is a ritual procedure in many traditions to perform this "calling down of the light", that is, the life force. In the Indian Upanishads it is called "milking the Sky Cow," in the Kabbalah and Golden Dawn "practicing the Middle Pillar," in Christianity "asking God for a blessing" (as in the "miracle of Pentecost"), in Wicca "drawing down the moon," and so on.

One can also perform this drawing down of the light as an independent meditation – it is extremely effective.

IX 5. k)   Fire and Light

Since the root chakra and the crown chakra are the two poles in the realm of proximity, contact, connection, etc., it is not surprising that there is a connection between calling the earth fire into the root chakra and calling the sky light into the crown chakra.

When the Kundalini has ascended to the crown, it calls down the sky light without any further action on the part of the meditator. The earth fire is primarily life force, but the sky light also has an integrating effect – the earth fire is closer to the body, the sky light is closer to the consciousness.

Therefore, the sky light, when it flows down through the chakras from above to below, does not cause a strengthening as is the case with the earth fire, but causes a joy. The various forms of joy that arise when the different chakras are integrated is a central element in Kundalini Yoga. This joy comes suddenly and with great force – you start to smile and then quite quickly you have this "Cheshire cat grin" on your face, which you can hardly defend yourself against. At the latest, when you have experienced this joy, you don't need any further impetus to sit down to meditate – it just feels too good …

Joy arises when several things start to vibrate together – either in the psyche (integration of a content of consciousness) or between oneself and a person or thing on the outside (meeting a friend).

The earth fire is mostly called "Kundalini" in India and the sky light "Bindhu". The joy is called "Ananda".

The rising earth fire and the descending sky light are the great flows of life force, into which the small convection current of the life force in man, of which Kundalini is a part, can insert and embed itself and by which it is nourished and enveloped.

When one includes this great, outer life-force flow in the meditations on one's own small, inner flow, the character of the meditation changes fundamentally – the experience becomes broader, more comprehensive, one experiences oneself as part of a greater whole …

IX 5. l)   Kundalini Deities

In this subject it becomes very individual – both in terms of the choice of the deity and the procedure.

Some deities associated with Kundalini are Re, Osiris and Uraeus (Egypt) Shiva, Buddha and the Nagas (India), Cernunnos (Celts), Sintela (Dakota), Quetzalcoatl (Toltecs, Aztecs, Mayas and others), dragons (Europe, India, China), etc.

One may e.g. make a dream journey to such a deity, one may ask her for help in a prayer, one may take her name as a Kundalini mantra, one may invoke her, i.e. identify oneself with her, etc.

More specific instructions on this subject may be found later in the chapter "Invocations".

IX 5. m) Rising of Kundalini

Unfortunately, one cannot say in general in which order one should use the methods given in this chapter – and for many of them one cannot even say exactly in which situation one should use them.

You can just start with a simple meditation and then see what happens. If nothing new happens, you can add one of the listed methods to your meditation and see what effect it has – or just meditate more often or longer.

With some methods, the effect can be predicted with some accuracy: the Sushumna stabilizes, the calling of the earth fire brings a strengthening, the calling of the sky light brings integration and joy, the invocation of a Kundalini deity brings a boost of intensity, dream journeys to the Kundalini bring clarification and stimulation, etc. How this works with a certain person, however, cannot be known in advance.

So one has rough clues, tries out and experiences and tries the next one – or simply stays for a year with a method that has proven itself and leads to interesting and beneficial experiences.

IX 6.   Duration and Frequency of Meditations

In several forms of meditation that have a relation to Kundalini, there is a hint that these meditations should be done daily for at least two years – possibly it takes a little longer until a fundamental transformation occurs. This duration is also confirmed by my own experience.

So you should be prepared for at least two years of meditation and leave the end open …

As with most things, there is no fixed rule for the duration of each meditation and the frequency of meditation per day. Fanatics say that you have to meditate very often and for a very long time, but I have also had pleasing results with meditation for 5 minutes 1-3 times a day. However, I may have benefited from the fact that I have meditated almost daily for more than 40 years – even though I have done many different meditations.

But as they say so aptly in the Rhineland, "Every Jeck is different." This also applies to meditation – "trial and error makes perfect." Trial and error is the only way to gain sure knowledge.

IX 7.   Dealing with the Effects of Meditation

Exactly which effects which meditation will have cannot be predicted with certainty. Nor can the effect of the actions one takes on the basis of the meditation experiences be predicted with certainty. Consequently, a "attitude in the face of the unpredictable" is needed.

IX 7. a)   Elastic Constancy

Elastic constancy is the foundation of any voyage of discovery in life – both external and internal voyages of discovery. This basic attitude involves many different aspects.

The first important point is not to give up in the face of difficulties, but to look at the difficulties – and remain kind to oneself: "look, feel, embrace."

It is equally important not to lose one's head when unexpected events occur or when violent feelings or pain arise, and not to fall into groundless fear.

Instead of stopping meditating completely when difficulties arise, it makes more sense to shorten or reduce the meditations, possibly sometimes also to increase them or to vary them. In this way, the "meditation thread" remains intact, but is allowed to change. In this way a living form of meditation emerges.

On the one hand, perseverance and consistency are a good foundation, but one should also spice it up with a pinch of experimentation and see what influence it has on the whole.

Meditation is usually something you have planned and know in advance what you are going to do, when and how. However, there are always unexpected situations and experiences in meditation, in which you have to see whether you simply continue with the plan or whether an improvisation would make more sense in the situation.

In general, one can say that one should not change a method with which one has arrived at a good state. As they say, "Never change a winning team!"

The living elasticity and elegance comes from a balance between the courage and adventurousness on one side and the caution and prudence on the other. In this balancing act, one gradually becomes more confident by practice.

If it is possible, one should also exchange ideas with others – with people who use the same method, but also with people who approach the whole thing completely differently. In this way, one avoids too much one-sidedness and comes up with one or two new ideas.

Finally, it makes sense to have some kind of emergency backup in case something goes thoroughly wrong. This can be a friend, a teacher, or anyone who is sufficiently knowledgeable on the subject.

IX 7. b)   Kindness

A very helpful attitude is kindness both to oneself and to the things one finds within oneself in meditation. This sounds very simple, but it is very effective: kindness relaxes inner conflicts, kindness is a first step towards integration, kindness is an approach to self-healing …

IX 7. c)   Look, Feel, Embrace

This process has been mentioned several times by now – it is the basic dynamic of healing.

The first step is <u>looking</u>: If one does not know and understand and fathom a thing, it is difficult to come into productive contact and exchange with it. Therefore, everything begins with perception, looking, observing. At first, one keeps the distance that is necessary in order to arrive at a neutral judgment that is as objective as possible.

This is the attitude of the sober scientist. In this step, strong feelings and panic reactions to what one has found within oneself and is now contemplating are an obstacle. Therefore, it makes sense to first take enough distance to oneself not to immediately evaluate everything, but to simply look at it objectively and to recognize the structures in what is being looked at, its origins, motives and effects.

One aspect of this step will be to recognize at what age the basis for what is being looked at was formed, i.e. one will see oneself at the age at which the examined imprinting took place.

The second step is <u>feeling</u>: When one begins to understand what is being looked at, one will realize how it has arisen in oneself. This creates, so to speak, compassion with oneself – one can not only understand what is going on in what is being looked at, but one can also feel what is going on.

At this point, in a first step, the "scientist" becomes a sympathetic friend. One, i.e. the "today's I" feels with a certain independence what one experienced and felt earlier, i.e. what the "young I" experienced and felt. This gives the old feelings the possibility to be there and to show themselves and to move more freely – they are now no longer lonely and locked up.

In this step, one faces oneself in a younger age, so to speak, and looks at one's counterpart with sympathy and understanding. At the same time, it is important not to fall into "pity", i.e. not to simply feel what the "younger self" feels or even to let these feelings swamp oneself. It is important to notice these feelings, but to remain steadfast and keep your head above water while doing so. It doesn't help to panic or become despondent – that will, at worst, lead to a reinforcement of the trauma. So: be kindly sympathetic to the feelings, but don't sink down into them.

The third step is <u>embracing</u>: By looking at the structures and perceiving the feelings, one now knows what one is facing and what motivation and intensity it has – one has gotten to know the unknown.

By this, one begins to see that what one is looking at is a part of oneself and that its root is ultimately one's own self-preservation. The thing under consideration is therefore not an enemy, but only a part of oneself that has lost its way and that has frozen in an attitude that today is more of a disadvantage than an advantage.

In this phase it is helpful to talk to the person under consideration (the "younger I"), to show him one's own good will and to help him to understand his own situation. This can be seen as a conversation with oneself – it also has great similarity with family constellations. During this step it becomes clearer and clearer that oneself and the thing being looked at are ultimately the same. The figurative form of this realization is the reflex that one embraces the "young self" as the "present self": one welcomes back what is being looked at, i.e. in most cases oneself as a child.

This is integration.

IX 7. d) Crises

The rising Kundalini will push against any blockage in the chakras and in the intermediate chakras, since they are on its path. Therefore, anything old that has not yet been healed will become conscious by the rising of the Kundalini. This is like a healing fever – the Kundalini is also heat. The crises caused by the rising Kundalini are the fever of healing.

One should dose the Kundalini in such a way that a slight fever arises and one can heal the old diseases, but one should do it so gently that, if possible, the healing process does not disturb or completely hinder one's daily life.

IX 7. e) Development in Waves

Developments do not proceed in a straight line, but in waves, in spurts, in a constant up and down – whereby the average of these waves gradually rises to a higher level.

If nothing new happens for a long time, if something becomes quite violent, or if one feels nothing at all for two weeks during meditation, one should not be alarmed: the development is so complex that it cannot be uniform at all.

This is due to the fact that a healing consists of various steps of cognition, feeling and action, that the astrological constellations are constantly changing, that there are constantly changing external circumstances, and that one's own soul also accompanies and partially directs the whole process – after all, the soul is interested in being able to radiate itself as unhindered as possible, for which the psyche must heal.

IX 8. Aids

Finally, there are two aids which are not very obvious at first:

One is homeopathy, which as an accompanying measure can help to heal old wounds and to discover, explore and practice new behaviors – this effect should not be underestimated.

The second help is osteopathy – since many old psychological wounds lead to bad posture, where the body is heavily stressed and the old feelings are trapped, healing one's own posture can make it much easier to dissolve the psychological blockages.

Of course, there are many other therapies, such as family constellations, which can also be helpful. In the case of physical ailments, a doctor may also be helpful. In the same way, astrology can help to find the crisis points in one's own biography and character and to outline new ways of behaving. Perhaps a firewalk is also useful to dissolve the sentence "I can't do that!" – or a sweat lodge to regain primal trust.

The individual path may look very different and contain many different elements.

IX 9. Ecstasy Methods

So far, mainly the meditative methods have been described – they are the ones most commonly used today. But there are also the ecstatic methods, which have been widely used especially in shamanism in the past.

The ecstatic methods have already been described in the chapter "VI 12". They consist of a concentration with the help of movements, which gradually increase and at the same time are firmly anchored in a rhythm, which gives support to the increase. These movements are usually a dance, which often includes stamping, and which in most cases repeats certain sequences of movements over and over again.

The drumming by which these dances are accompanied, or which is sometimes itself the ecstasy movement, evokes a force that carries the drumming and the consciousness. This is an effect that is difficult to describe. It usually occurs after the first few notes – then you know that you are in contact with something greater, which then fills the drumming and captivates your own consciousness and also that of the listeners. In this kind of drumming, something is present in the room that everyone can feel. Sometimes this something is also present in music that has been recorded on CDs – but this is rare. This something is also not limited to drumming, although it seems to occur most easily there. This something can be found with any instrument.

Sometimes the ecstasy methods are accompanied by loudly spoken mantras, hymns and chanting. Chanting, in particular, can also be the central ecstasy method itself, that is, what you get into the rhythm.

Finally, there is hyperventilation as a method of ecstasy. It is suitable for raising the vital force level and thereby dissolving blockages: however, it is a sometimes rather violent and unspecific method, which needs as a supplement a method by which that, what one has experienced in hyperventilation, is integrated.

IX 10. The Universal Kundalini

Kundalini" in the previous considerations has always meant the ascending part of the life-force circulation in one's own body. However, there is also the idea of a universal Kundalini, i.e. a life force in the whole world and a life force flow in it.

In this context, there are various ideas and images about the Kundalini:

    - the Kundalini as a snake-shaped goddess,
    - the Kundalini as the life force in all things, and
      - the Kundalini as the ascending force and the Bindhu as the descending force.

This concept is very similar to the concept of an omnipresent prana ("life force") – but in the concept of a Kundalini goddess, the life force is conceived and personified as being aware of itself.

Similar concepts exist among many peoples. For example, the Egyptian "ankh" is also the life force, the Wakan Tanka ("Great Mystery") of the Dakotas is an all-encompassing and conscious life force, the Holy Spirit in Christianity is, so to speak, "God's life force" …

The important point about universal Kundalini is above all the insight that the flow of life force in one's own body is not an isolated phenomenon, but is in exchange with the flow of life force in all things.

The connection between the individual Kundalini and universal Kundalini is the same as that between subconsciousness and collective subconsciousness, or between inner images and telepathy, or between physical actions and telekinesis.

One may consider just the inner processes, but the picture becomes more complete, if one considers also the relations to the outside – no matter whether one calls these relations life force threads, telepathy, universal Kundalini, Holy Spirit or any other name.

In the awakening of Kundalini, these life-force connections to the outside occur, for example, in the light ray to the glowing centre of the earth, in the light ray to the celestial light, in Shiva invocations or in common ecstasies. However, it can be assumed that these connections have an effect on the processes of meditation or ecstasy even when they are not specifically used or imagined.

IX 10. a)   Flow of Kundalini

If one looks more closely at the flow of Kundalini, a peculiarity stands out.

Self-contained systems have an inner circuit that leads from a center outward and then back to the center: in humans and animals, blood flows from the heart through the veins outward to the head, fingers, and toes, and then back to the heart; in the sun, matter is heated in the center by nuclear fusion, rises to the surface, cools there, and then sinks back down.

Open systems that receive influences from outside have a flow instead of a circuit, with vortices forming along this flow: a stream flowing through a pond; or the digestive system of humans and animals (mouth – throat – stomach – intestine – anus).

Since the Kundalini rises from below from the root chakra through all seven chakras and leaves them again above through the crown chakra, the Kundalini must be a passage flow.

The structure of the chakras, on the other hand, is a central system with a convection current: the heart chakra in the center, which expresses itself with the help of the three outer pairs of chakras in three stages (impulse – structure – contact).

The flow of the life force in the form of Kundalini through the life force body thus does not correspond to the blood circulation, but to the digestive tract. However, there are two forms of nourishment in humans: before birth by an external impulse (by the mother) through the umbilical cord, and after the birth by its own impulse through the mouth.

Kundalini seems to be a form of life force nourishment of the body. The question is whether the life force body actively sucks in life force through the root chakra or whether it is passively nourished with life force through this chakra.

First of all, in meditation one can observe that although there is slurping meditation, it is also possible to simply open the root chakra to the incoming life force without consciously "sucking" it in. However, this is not yet a definite proof that the life force body is passively nourished, but it is at least a proof that there is a dynamic in the life force that ensures that one is supplied with life force – whether one absorbs it unconsciously or whether one receives it sent, is still unclear for the time being. Maybe there are both – like breastfeeding a child, where the breasts secrete the milk and the child absorbs the milk.

IX 10. b)   Life Force Umbilical Cord

Where does the life force that flows into the body through the root chakra come from? It definitely comes from outside the body. It can be assumed that it is not drawn from a particular person, animal, plant, or the like – the source will probably be the earth.

This leads to the image of an umbilical cord to the earth, through which life force flows from the earth to the individual. This creates either a nourishment of the individual with life force (should humans need replenishment of life force) or merely an exchange of life force with the earth (taking in life force through the root chakra and giving out life force through the crown chakra).

The imagination of this umbilical cord from the root chakra to the earth has proven to be extremely helpful in Kundalini meditation.

With the help of this umbilical cord one can also consecrate places in energetic Feng Shui, i.e. charge them with the life force that arises out of the core of the earth.

This life force umbilical cord is therefore a meaningful concept and a meaningful imagination – simply because it is extremely effective.

IX 10. c)   Heart Chakra of the Earth

In meditation, it has been shown that the imagination of this life-force umbilical cord is most effective when it is imagined down into the glowing iron/nickel core of the earth. When one imagines a ray of light from the root chakra down to the center of the earth and invites the life force to ascend, this life force usually ascends into one's body in the form of a serpent or dragon.

If one undertakes a dream journey to the center of the earth, one can find there a large "glow amoeba" which has approximately the shape of a slipper animalcule, that is, it looks like a slightly oval lens which is a little dented in its center. The shape of this being is also very similar to red blood cells. This "glow amoeba" is the most powerful thing I have encountered so far.

It would be obvious to understand this "glow amoeba" as the root chakra of the earth, which connects with the root chakras of humans and animals (and plants?) via the life force umbilical cord. However, the center of a galaxy, a sun, a planet or a moon is its heart chakra, because it is precisely the center of the system concerned. Also from the center of the earth hot lava rises and forms then volcanoes and causes the continental drift – at the same time cooled down substance sinks deeper into the earth. The center of this convection current in the earth is its iron/nickel core. This core is obviously the heart chakra of the earth.

The life force ist the border between consciousness and matter – thus there should be not only uprising matter (lava) in the earth but also uprising life force. This uprising life force is the flow that can be seen as one's own dragon that is uprising out of the earth and then rising inside one's body as Kundalini. So the earth is sending up life force into the human body – and one's own "sucking life force" in meditation is just a help in taking this life force send up by the earth.

The earth has a convection current of lava and thus also of life force – each human has a convection current and life force of blood. The lava-current of the earth is an analogy to the convection current of blood in man. The life force convection current of the earth nourishes the life force body of man – this appeares as the Kundalini in man. The life force current of the earth rises up out of the earth – this upward flow continues in man as the uprising Kundalini that enters by the root chakra and leaves by the crown chakra.

Thus the earth is nourishing the life force body on man and also of animals and plants and fungi – and most probably the life force flow of the earth connects man to earth, which means that there is also a flow of information from the earth to man (entering at the root chakra) and from man back to the earth (leaving at the crown chakra).

IX 10. d) Gaia

Life force is ultimately just the direct conscious perception of the transition between consciousness and matter.

This means that a life force umbilical cord from man to earth also connects the consciousness of man with the consciousness of earth.

Since all people have a life force umbilical cord to the earth, the consciousnesses, i.e. the subconsciousnesses of the people are connected to each other by the earth. From this it follows that the collective subconsciousness, which consists of the telepathic coupling of all the subconsciousnesses of mankind, is very probably located in the earth.

The collective subconscious contains as "units" the deities. This means that the life force umbilical cord to the earth is also the access to the deities. It further means that for the "extraordinary magic" (miracles) for which the contact with the Deities is necessary, the awareness of this umbilical cord to the earth is required. It is consistent with this that for the "extraordinary magic", as a rule, the awakening of the Kundalini is required.

Since on earth, besides human beings, there are animals, plants and fungi, "Gaia" as the consciousness of the Earth, is more than just the collective subconsciousness of human beings. In Gaia are also the collective subconsciousnesses of all species of animals, plants and fungi – and possibly also of all species of minerals.

These connections have been explored little or not at all. However, the use of this life force umbilical cord in meditation shows that it can play a decidedly important element in the awakening of Kundalini.

This umbilical cord is the supply of the life force, the connection to the collective subconsciousness, and the connection to the gods.

(A more detailed presentation of the different forms of consciousness from the waking consciousness of man to the collective subconsciousness and to Gaia may be found in my two books "Life Force for Beginners" and "Da'ath Magic for Beginners").

IX 10. e)   Two Systems of Life Force Currents

There is one current of life force that is an analogy to the digestion system: Life force rises out of the earth into the root chakra, rises further up to the crown chakra and leaves the body there. This ist the "Kundalini current".

The other current of life force is an analogy to the system of the blood circulation. In this system, that includes the acupuncture meridians, informations flow from the the heart chakra into the whole body and also from the whole body back to the heart chakra. This ist the "Heart chakra current".

The Kundalini current is part of the "body foreign" processes. This current is in analogy to the mouth, the throat, the stomach, the guts and the anus. It contains "body foreign" substances (nourishment).

The Heart chakra current is part of the "body own" processes. This current is in analogy to the blood, the limbs, the organs and the brain. It consists of "body own" substances like bone, flesh, skin and blood.

The soul in the heart chakra is the centre of the "body defining" processes. This part of the life force body is in analogy to the cell nuclei and the genitals. It consists of "body defining" substances and of the organs belonging to them like cell nuclei, DNA, sperm, penis, ovum and uterus.

IX 10. f) Light and Fire

The life force, that is rising in the earth and after this out of the earth, is seen and felt as fire – the Kundalini.

Indian yogis often describe another flow of life force, that comes down from above. This flow is seen as white light – therefore in the Upanishads the calling down of this flow is called "milking the sky cow". This light is often called "Bindhu".

The downflow of the light usually is started by letting the Kundalini rise to the crown chakra. Nevertheless it is possible to call down this light without awakening the Kundalini beforehand. This "calling down of the light" usually is done by prayer, concentration or ritual – for example by Christian mystics (prayer) or by witches ("drawing down the moon").

It is possible to describe the chakras as different mixtures of fire and light:

Crown chakra: 0/6 fire – 0/6 light
=> awareness, consciousness, presence, perception

Third Eye: 1/6 fire – 5/6 light
=> directed attention, concentration, alignment

Throat Chakra: 2/6 fire - 4/6 light
=> conscious creation, community, self-expression

Heart Chakra: 3/6 fire – 3/6 light
=> center, balance, identity, "temple of the soul"

Solar Plexus: 4/6 fire – 2/6 light
=> directed power, mobility, invigoration, connection

Hara: 5/6 fire – 1/6 light
=> centered power, inner support, steadfastness, rhythm

Root Chakra: 6/6 fire – 0/6 light
=> vitality, instincts, will to live, needs, power

The fire of Kundalini is the life force that is radiated outwards by the earth – but what is the light, thar shines downwards onto the earth?

It could be the life force of the earth, that is returning to the earth – i.e. the other part, the downwards part of the convection flow of the life force of the earth. But this would not expain the quite different quality of the downwards flowing light compared to the upwards rising fire.

There is another possible explanation: The light could be the life force of the sun that reaches the earth.

This would fit well:

- The rising fire ist the analogy of the warmth of the earth. The temperature of the earth is about 300° above absolute zero (-273°C). Warmth is a kind of fire. It rises from below.

- The sun is radiating light and warmth. So it is fitting to see and feel the life force of the sun as light. It descends from above.

This fits well with the symbolism of the sweat lodge: Below is Grandmother Earth, who gives heat (fire) with the glowing stones in the centre of the sweat lodge. Above is Grandfather Sun (or Grandfather Sky) who gives the light of the sun. Grandmother Earth gives confidence as a present to man – Grandfather Sun gives responsibilitiy as a present to man.

So there seems to be a complex system of radiating systems, that all contain a convection current:

Order of Radiating Systems						
System	*convection current*		*centre*		*seen on earth as*	
	matter	*life force*	*matter*	*life force*	*matter*	*life force*
galaxy	gravitation	?	black hole	God?	?	?
sun	"sun-lava"	light	atomic fusion in centre	sun-god?	light, heat, magnetic field	light from above = Bindhu
earth	"earth lava"	warmth	heat by pressure	"red blood cell" being = Gaia?	warmth, magnetic field	fire from below
man	blood circulation	radiating from the heart and retur-ning to the heart	heart	soul	digestive system	heat from below = Kundalini

The <u>fundamental system</u> is the galaxy, but on the life force effects of the whole galaxy or of the black hole in its centre hardly anything can be said.

The <u>second system</u> is the sun. The "heart of the sun" ist the atomic fusion in its centre, which causes the sun to shine and to radiate heat. The shape of the life force heart of the sun is not known as far as I know. The life force, that belongs to the light and heat, that is radiated by the sun, is seen as white light (Bindhu), that has the quality of integration and joy in meditation.

The third system is the earth. The "heart of the earth" is the white-hot glowing iron/nickel core of the earth. The life force heart of the earth is the thing that is seen as a large glowing red blood cell in meditaion and on dream journeys – probably this is the heart of Gaia. The life force that belongs to this rising heat is experienced as a rising fire in meditation.

The fourth system is man. His heart is his physical heart and his life force heart is his heart chakra, that may also be called sun chakra. In this chakra the soul lives as in a temple. The rising life force of the earth is experienced as the rising Kundalini fire inside one's own body – and the downflowing life force of the sun is experienced as the Bindhu light inside one's own body.

IX 10. g) Zodiac

The life force of the earth and presumbly every sun, planet and moon has another strukture: the Zodiac. This is the foundation of the cycles astrology.

Maybe this structure could also be used for the awakening of the Kundalini but so far I don't know of any tactic that uses this structure.

The Zodiac is a twelve-part circle – and the heart chakra has twelve petals. If there is a reliable conection betwen both is doubtful – maybe this is just a coincidence of numbers.

IX 10. h) Places of Power

Places of power and also ley lines are structures in the life force body of the earth. Maybe they could also be used to awaken the Kundalini. At least meditation on volcanoes furthers the rising of life force in one's own body.

X   Rituals

A ritual is a mostly largely fixed course of action, the goal of which is the movement of the life force. Broadly speaking, a meditation can also be considered a ritual, but in a narrower sense a ritual consists of gestures that illustrate the inner images by which one directs the life force. A simple form of a ritual is, for example, the laying on of hands during a blessing, by which the imagination of the flow of the life force from the deity through the priest to the blessed is supported and made visible to all.

Such rituals can also be used for the awakening of Kundalini.

X 1.   Invocations

In an invocation, one usually identifies with a deity. In the context of Kundalini, these are the gods in whose myths Kundalini plays an important role, such as Shiva, Buddha and Cernunnos (Celts), or deities that have evolved from the ideas about Kundalini, such as Sintela (Dakota), Quetzalcoatl (Toltecs, Aztecs, Mayans, etc.) or the two serpents on the Caduceus-staff of Hermes (Greeks).

The difference between an invocation and a dream journey has two aspects in terms of procedure: First, in a dream journey one sees the images internally and in an invocation externally, and second, in a dream journey one usually approaches one's goal slowly, while in an invocation this happens rather quickly. A dream journey is usually used when you want to get to know something – with an invocation you already know where you want to go (although an invocation can sometimes have something of an uncertain journey of discovery).

An invocation has three steps:

> 1st step: One imagines the figure of the deity before oneself. Beforehand, one will usually have familiarized oneself with the deity by contemplating the traditional images, statues, myths, etc. of this deity. Possibly one has already undertaken dream journeys to it.
>
> One begins to describe the deity – both its figure and its symbols and rudimentarily also its myths.
>
> In doing so, one speaks in the distanced form: "She is … She has … She does …"
>
> One creates clarity.

2nd step: One goes towards the imagined figure of the deity and feels in oneself the longing for the connection with this deity.

One begins to describe especially the myths of this deity, that is, its abilities and activities, as well as what one hopes to receive from it and the reason why one is performing this invocation. One's own language becomes much more emotional than in the rather factual and neutral first step.

In doing so, one addresses the deity directly: "You are … You have … You do …"

One creates a connection.

3rd step: One enters into the imagined figure and identifies with it and feels it in one's whole body and takes on the form of the deity in one's own imagination.

One begins to speak as the deity itself, i.e. one imagines speaking as it. In doing so, one's speech may become increasingly free and improvisational, in order to give the deity the opportunity to speak through oneself.

In doing so, one speaks as the deity: "I am … I have … I do …"

One creates an identity with the deity.

Finally, one steps back out of the deity and does what seems appropriate – giving thanks, grounding oneself, contemplating the experience, etc.

One can perform an invocation simply to experience the deity (mysticism), but also to obtain more of its properties and abilities (healing, development) or to achieve something specific with its help (magic).

The three steps of invocation correspond to the method "look, feel, embrace":

- look   = describe the deity factually
- feel   = to establish an emotional connection with the deity
- embrace   = identify oneself with the deity, integrate oneself into it

Consequently, the healing and the invocation are analogous processes: something that has been separate before is first looked at, then connected with and finally united.

This process shows that there is also a difference in the result between a dream journey and an invocation: The dream journey usually consists only of a contemplation, which can sometimes lead to an emotional touching, while the invocation leads to identification by contemplation and feelings. Of course, it is possible to identify oneself with one's own power animal or with one's own soul during a dream journey, and it is also possible to perform an invocation during a dream journey, but this happens quite rarely and is not a common part of a dream journey.

An invocation starting from a dream journey has the advantage that on it one can usually see the imagined images that appeared by themselves more clearly and vividly – but it also has the disadvantage that one does not make any physical movements during the invocation and usually also does not speak aloud, which both ground the experience.

X 2. Kundalini Invocations

During an invocation, as already stated, one usually identifies with a deity. Since the inner Kundalini is already a part of oneself, in contact with the inner Kundalini, dream journeys are more appropriate than invocations, that is, identification with a greater and external being.

One could only invoke the outer, universal Kundalini, but since one's own Kundalini is a part of the outer Kundalini, a dream journey to the universal Kundalini seems to be more appropriate here as well. On such a dream journey one can expand one's own Kundalini into the universal Kundalini.

Of course, there is nothing to be said against invoking the outer, universal Kundalini with a ritual invocation.

X 3. Tantra

The healed inner man and the healed inner woman are on the one hand connected with Ida and Pingala and on the other hand of course closely connected with sexuality, which in turn is one of the most important effects of Kundalini in the psyche. Therefore, there is also the possibility of using sexuality and thus the two aforementioned inner images to awaken the Kundalini.

There are three different starting points from which to build and perform such a "Kundalini ritual".

X 3. a) Inner Ritual

This ritual is basically a meditation. However, since these inner images have a somewhat more complex dynamic, it can also be called an "inner ritual". This meditation ritual has been largely described in an earlier chapter.

The process itself is very simple: the inner whole man and the inner whole woman unite with each other. However, this process can be made more complex in different ways. You should choose the complexity that suits you the most – complex or simple is not better, it is just different.

- One can imagine the process of union completely formless, making it more or less a dream journey in which one is largely a spectator and very little a ritual leader.

- One can choose a particular posture such as the one called "Yab-Yum" in Tibet. In this, the man sits in the lotus position and the woman sits on his lap and crosses her legs behind his back. As a man, one would take the role of the man in Yab-Yum – as a woman the role of the woman.

- One can imagine the union in the "Yab-Yum" posture on the lotus of the root chakra.

- One can imagine the union in the "Yab-Yum" posture on the lotus flowers of all seven chakras simultaneously.

- One can also consider the different qualities of the union of the whole inner man and the whole inner woman in the seven main chakras:
> - the pair of life force fullness in the root chakra,
> - the pair of inner hold and life dance in the hara,
> - the pair of physical self-expression and radiance in the solar plexus,
> - the pair of identity and thus the mirror images of the soul in the heart chakra,
> - the pair of social self-expression and self-confidence in the throat chakra,
> - the pair of clarity, orientation, and purpose in the third eye, and finally
> - the pair of all-connectedness and enlightenment in the crown chakra.

- Instead of the seven main chakras, one may also imagine the two figures in Ida and Pingala, which then become the Sushumna by their union.

Here there are hardly any limits to one's own creativity.

X 3. b)   External Life Force Ritual

The external life force ritual is so simple that at first glance one might think that it is just boring and that nothing can happen. It consists of a man and woman uniting physically, but then moving only as much as is necessary to keep the erotic tension from dropping completely. Instead of wanting to increase the tension, both are simply attentive to what is happening in their own bodies.

By maintaining the erotic tension by occasional movements, there is a constant pressure on the life force in the root chakra – there is a tense and at the same time relaxed concentration in the root chakra, i.e. a powerful but relaxed concentration.

Since this tension is not released by an orgasm and thus not discharged in the usual way in the root chakra, the life force seeks another way – and this leads upward through the Sushumna as well as through Ida and Pingala. This rising of the life force is the Kundalini.

So this method is ultimately a concentration on the root chakra with the help of eroticism. Since the erotic and sexual are something that most people can focus on very easily, this is a method that facilitates concentration for most people.

The difficulty with this method in the beginning is not to switch from "tantra mode" to "normal sexuality" with the pursuit of orgasm.

X 3. c)   External Image Ritual

One can also perform the inner union of the whole inner man with the whole inner woman externally as a ritual and stimulate the inner process by its external representation.

For this, as a man, one has to identify the woman who participates in this ritual with one's own whole inner woman, or as a woman, one has to identify the man who participates in this ritual with one's own whole inner man.

It is obvious that after the ritual it is necessary to take back the projection: It is not particularly desirable to confuse a real woman with one's own whole inner woman – the same is true for the whole inner man.

Ultimately, every time you love someone, the loved one is associated with the whole inner man or woman – this is how love is created. So this ritual is not an unusual or even unnatural process – but you should still handle all kinds of identifications with a bit of sensitivity, otherwise they can create confusion.

In this ritual one identifies an inner image with an outer person – a projection. In invocation, one identifies a deity with oneself – an introjection. If one uses both consciously and also dissolves them afterwards, these methods can be very helpful, but it is important that one uses them as consciously as possible.

X 3. d)   Ritual of the Relationship Mandala

This ritual consists of seven steps.

- In the <u>first step,</u> one searches within oneself for the two polarized inner male images and the two polarized inner female images. The three possible polarizations are the already mentioned pairs "addict – ascetic," "perpetrator – victim," and "star – fan."

- In the <u>second step,</u> you look at which image you yourself perform in your life, and which images three other people perform for you. These three others take on the role of relationship partner, the role of friend, and the role of enemy. For example, in the case of a he-addict, the relationship partner is a she-ascetic, the enemy is a he-ascetic, and the friend is an she-addict. Another he-addict may be a "fellow sufferer" or a friend.

- In the <u>third step,</u> one places these four persons around oneself and realizes that they correspond to one's own inner images and are a part of oneself.

- In the <u>fourth step,</u> one dissolves one of the pairs (e.g. he-addict and he-ascetic) and thus finds again the first intact inner image.

- In the <u>fifth step,</u> one dissolves the other pair and thus finds again the second healthy inner image.

- In the <u>sixth step,</u> the whole inner man and the whole inner woman unite, revealing one's own soul in the center of the mandala.

- In the <u>seventh step</u> one lets one's own soul radiate through one's own psyche in all directions.

The complete and detailed description of this ritual can be found in my book "Das Beziehungs-Mandala". The complete description of this ritual would take up too much space in this book. In addition, although this ritual is a promotion of the awakening of Kundalini, it has no direct relation to Kundalini – it is more of an indirect aid to the rising of the Kundalini.

XI Siddhis

By awakening the Kundalini, blockages in the chakras and thus in the psyche are usually dissolved. This allows the life force to flow freely again – and also the Kundalini, which is part of the life force, to flow freely in one's own body.

There are, of course, as always, exceptions to this rule, e.g. in the case of the short, violent rising of the Kundalini, in the case of the rising of the Kundalini with the help of drugs, in the case of the rising of the Kundalini accompanied by the perception of one's own fears, addictions and pains, etc. But in general, the pursuit of the Kundalini rising triggers a gradual dissolution of one's blockages.

Such a dissolution of the blockages leads to a new basic attitude. Before, one was fixated on the solid, rigid, hard, delimiting, holding on and clinging – afterwards, one is oriented towards the flowing, soft, elastic, elegant, connecting and affirming.

This transition is also described by Buddha in his writings as the attainment of the four boundaryless qualities of an enlightened one: boundless serenity, boundless compassion, boundless love, and boundless joy. In this state, there is no longer any delimitation to the outside world – identity is no longer based on delimitation, but on the perception of one's own quality.

> - The boundless serenity arises when one recognizes that everything consists of exchange processes.
> This corresponds to "looking".

> - The boundless compassion arises from the fact that one emotionally participates in everything else – a logical consequence of the boundless serenity, by which one can see things as they really are … just everything connected with each other.
> This corresponds to "feeling".

> - The boundless love arises from the fact that due to the boundless compassion one wants to care for the other as much as for oneself – one is also the other.
> This corresponds to "embracing."

> - Boundless joy arises from the dissolution of demarcation and from swinging together, because this "swinging together" is what joy is.
> This corresponds to the effect of "look, feel, embrace".

Consequently, the awakening of Kundalini leads to a different state of consciousness, to a different attitude in life.

This development is also described in other systems such as the Kabbalistic Tree of

Life. There the Kundalini appears as the "snake of wisdom", which ascends from the bottom to the top. The lowest area ("Malkuth") represents the body, the following seven areas ("Yesod" to "Da'ath") the seven main chakras and the three uppermost areas ("Binah" to "Kether") the unity underlying everything.

In the Indian scriptures it is reported in very many places that by the awakening of the Kundalini also new abilities arise, which are called "Siddhis", which could be translated as "magical abilities". These abilities are also described by the Kabbalists of reaching Da'ath and in the Bible they are found as miracles.

These abilities are more or less unlimited and include multiplying loaves of bread, turning water into wine, drinking poison or liquid copper without harm, walking on water, curing diseases, raising the dead, telepathy, telekinesis, seeing and walking through walls, levitating and levitating oneself (levitation), being able to fast indefinitely, ceasing to breathe for several hours or days, ending the need for sleep, and so on. This list could be continued for a long time.

Now, of course, this does not mean that everyone who has awakened their Kundalini will have all these abilities, but awakening the Kundalini can lead to one or another of these abilities. It is different for everybody, because everybody is different – from his soul, from his psyche, from his horoscope and so on.

The awakening of the Kundalini is also interesting in itself, but actually it is not an end in itself, but leads to self-healing. This is associated with a new attitude towards life and also with new abilities. This new attitude towards life is what it is all about – what Buddha calls "boundless joy", what in India is called "Ananda", what inAncient Egypt was called "hotep" and what in Christianity is roughly described as "bliss".

This attitude towards life leads to a quiet smile as in the Buddha statues or in the statues from ancient Egypt – with a somewhat more fiery temperament, this new attitude towards life can also lead to a "Cheshire cat grin".

This is what is actually valuable to be found by the awakening of Kundalini.

English Books by Harry Eilenstein

- Living Magic (261 p.)
- The Synthesis of Physics and Magic (192 p.)
- Telepathy for Beginners (60 p.)
- Telepathy for Advanced Learners (52 p.)
- Telekinesis for Beginners (56 p.)
- Life Force for Beginners (76 p.)
- Kundalini for Beginners (104 p.)
- Astral Projection for Beginners (60 p.)
- Meditation for Beginners (60 p.)
- Prophecy for Beginners (60 p.)
- Ritual Magic for Beginners (64 p.)
- Magic Chant for Beginners (108 p.)
- Invocations for Beginners (52 p.)
- Evocations for Beginners (62 p.)
- Auto-Movement for Beginners (60 p.)
- Elves for Beginners (56 p.)
- Hypnosis for Beginners (56 p.)
- Love Magic for Beginners (52 p.)
- Money Magic for Beginners (60 p.)

- Magic Objects for Beginners (64 p.)
- Shamanism for Beginners (52 p.)
- Chakra-Magic for Beginners (148 p.)
- Language of the Moon – for Beginners (128 p.)
- Self Knowledge for Beginners (60 p.)
- Da'ath-Magic for Beginners (64 p.)
- Astrology for Beginners (112 p.)
- Number Symbolism for Beginners (64 p.)
- Mandalas for Beginners (76 p.)
- Crop Circles for Beginners (344 p.)
- Feng Shui for Beginners (96 p.)
- Magic Research for Beginners (140 p.)

These books will be puplished soon:

- Magic for Beginners – Anthology I
- Magic for Beginners – Anthology II
- Magic for Beginners – Anthology III
- Magic for Beginners – Anthology IV

Bücher von Harry Eilenstein

Religion allgemein
- Die sieben Schritte des Lebens (428 S.)
- Muttergöttin und Schamanen (168 S.)
- Göbekli Tepe (472 S.)
- Die Göttin von Göbekli Tepe (144 S.)
- Die Biographie des Teufels (144 S.)
- Totempfähle (440 S.)
- Christus (60 S.)
- Dakini (80 S.)
- Vajra (76 S.)

Ägypten
- Hathor und Re 1: Götter und Mythen im Alten Ägypten (432 S.)
- Hathor und Re 2: Die altägyptische Religion – Ursprünge, Kult und Magie (396 S.)
- Isis (508 S.)

Indogermanen
- Die Entwicklung der indogermanischen Religionen (700 S.)
- Wurzeln und Zweige der indogermanischen Religion (224 S.)

Germanen
- Die Götter der Germanen (87 Bände – siehe nächste Seite)
- Odin (300 S.)

Kelten
- Cernunnos (690 S.)
- Taliesin (228 S.)
- Der Kessel von Gundestrup (220 S.)
- Der Chiemsee-Kessel (76)

Psychologie
- Über die Freude (100 S.)
- Das Geheimnis des inneren Friedens (252 S.)
- Das Beziehungsmandala (52 S.)
- Gefühle und ihre Verwandlungen (404 S.)
- einsgerichtet (140 S.)
- Liebe und Eigenständigkeit (216 S.)
- Von innerer Fülle zu äußerem Gedeihen (52 S.)

Heilung
- Die Symbolik der Krankheiten (76 S.)

Kunst
- Herz des Tanzes – Tanz des Herzens (160 S.)

Drama
- König Athelstan (104 S.)

Bücher von Harry Eilenstein

„Magie für Anfänger"	Magie

„Magie für Anfänger"

- Telepathie für Anfänger (60 S.)
- Telepathie für Fortgeschrittene (52 S.)
- Telekinese für Anfänger (52 S.)
- Lebenskraft für Anfänger (60 S.)
- Meditation für Anfänger (56 S.)
- Kundalini für Anfänger (100 S.)
- Hypnose für Anfänger (56 S.)
- Auto-Movement für Anfänger (56 S.)
- Chakra-Magie für Anfänger (148 S.)
- Astralreisen für Anfänger (56 S.)
- Astrologie für Anfänger (120 S.)
- Ritual-Magie für Anfänger (56 S.)
- Mandalas für Anfänger (68 S.)
- Geldzauber für Anfänger (56 S.)
- Liebeszauber für Anfänger (52 S.)
- Invokationen für Anfänger (52 S.)
- Evokationen für Anfänger (60 S.)
- Elfen für Anfänger (56 S.)
- Magie-Forschung für Anfänger (140 S.)
- Selbsterkenntnis für Anfänger (52 S.)
- Zahlensymbolik für Anfänger (60 S.)
- Die Sprache des Mondes – für Anfänger (116 S.)
- Zaubergesänge für Anfänger (100 S.)
- Zukunftschau für Anfänger (60 S.)
- Schamanismus für Anfänger (52 S.)
- Magische Gegenstände für Anfänger (68 S.)
- Da'ath-Magie für Anfänger (64 S.)
- Kornkreise für Anfänger (348 S.)
- Feng Shui für Anfänger (96 S.)
- Magie für Anfänger – Sammelband I (696 S.)
- Magie für Anfänger – Sammelband II (664 S.)
- Magie für Anfänger – Sammelband III (580 S.)

„Traumreisen"

- Traumreisen zu Heilpflanzen (700 S.)

Magie

- Handbuch für Zauberlehrlinge (408 S.)
- Tarot (104 S.)
- Physik und Magie (184 S.)
- Die Synthese von Physik und Magie (200S.)
- Die Magie-Formel (156 S.)
- Krafttiere – Tiergöttinnen – Tiertänze (112 S.)
- Schwitzhütten (524 S.)
- Mythen und Magie der Harfe (116 S.)
- Magie heute – Berichte aus der Praxis (288 S.)

Meditation

- Der Lebenskraftkörper (230 S.)
- Die Chakren (100 S.)
- Das Chakren-System mit den Nebenchakren (296 S.)
- Organe und Chakren (64 S.)
- Die platonischen Körper in den Chakren (156 S.)
- Meditation (140 S.)
- Drachenfeuer (124 S.)
- Kundalini I (676 S.)
- Reinkarnation (156 S.)
- einsgerichtet (140 S.)

Astrologie

- Astrologie (496 S.)
- Photo-Astrologie (428 S.)
- Die astrologischen Aspekte (88 S.)
- Horoskop und Seele (120 S.)

Kabbala

- Kursus der praktischen Kabbala (150 S.)
- Eltern der Erde (450 S.)
- Blüten des Lebensbaumes:
    - Die Struktur des kabbalistischen Lebensbaumes (370 S.)
    - Der kabbalistische Lebensbaum als Forschungshilfsmittel (580 S.)
    - Der kabbalistische Lebensbaum als spirituelle Landkarte (520 S.)

Die Themen der 87 Bände der Reihe „Die Götter der Germanen"